CHRISTIANITY

IN THE UNITED STATES

CHRISTIANITY

IN THE UNITED STATES

A Historical Survey and Interpretation

DAVID W. WILLS

University of Notre Dame Press   *Notre Dame, Indiana*

Library of Congress Cataloging-in-Publication Data
Wills, David W.
Christianity in the United States : a historical survey
David W. Wills.
   p. cm.
Includes bibliographical references and index.
ISBN 978-0-268-04406-0 **(paperback)**
   1. United States—Church history. 2. Christianity—
3. African Americans—Religion. I. Title.
br515.w49 2005

To my grandparents

David Edwards Wood (1885 – 1949)

Jessie Aird Wood (1882 – 1975)

and

the parents of my father, whose names

I do not know

Contents

Preface

This brief survey of the history of Christianity in the United States was originally written in the spring and summer of 2002 for publication in German in the *Theologische Realenzyklopädie* (TRE), an extraordinary multivolume reference work that is less well-known in the United States than it deserves to be. Published in Berlin by Verlag Walter de Gruyter under the general editorship of Gerhard Müller and now running to more than thirty volumes, the TRE includes, along with much, much else, substantial articles on the history and present circumstances of Christianity in many individual nations. The present work was commissioned as one such "Länderartikel," and appears in vol. 34, pp. 593–639, under the title "Vereinigte Staaten von Amerika." My assignment was not to survey American religion in general, but specifically to discuss Christianity in the United States. It was called to my attention that the TRE had already published, in its second volume, an article on "Amerikanische Religionen," so that Native American religion was not within the scope of my responsibilities. I was also asked to provide a brief overview of the contemporary denominational landscape, with some relevant statistics, and to supply a modest bibliography. The present work conforms to those specifications. Here and there I have revised or added a few sentences, or altered the section breaks and headings originally introduced by the TRE editors. Slightly to ease the path of the general reader, here approaching this piece without the massive explanatory cross-referencing provided by the TRE, I have added (albeit very sparingly and mostly in the early pages) an occasional footnote, which I hope will provide simple explanations of a few of the many theological terms, names of religious movements, and organizational titles that appear without explanation in the main body of the text. I have also included in the bibliography a few works that have been published within the last year. Otherwise the text published here closely follows the original German publication. I have not, for example, altered it to take fuller account of Christianity's development among American Indians.

Given the circumstances of its original publication, this work inevitably has a certain "encyclopedic" quality. It aims to provide, within a relatively short compass, a considerable amount of factual information, particularly with regard to the ever-growing diversity within the world of American Protestantism. It is hardly, however, a comprehensive charting of Christian variety in the United States. Little is said, for example, of the role the many different religious orders have played in advancing different styles of Catholic piety. And many individual groups go unmentioned. Though much attention is here given to religious diversity, this work is not intended *primarily* as a study in American pluralism. Religious pluralism, as both an ever-changing reality and an always-contested concept, is certainly one of the central themes in the religious history of the United States. But so too is the equally ever-changing and always-contested ways in which Christian groups have pursued a "holy commonwealth" in America. Of comparably weighty significance is the ongoing story of religion's place in this nation's still unresolved effort to come to terms with the realities of race. I wish to be *emphatic* about this point. The encounter of black and white within the history of American Christianity can neither be reduced to a mere instance of the larger question of religious pluralism nor can it be set aside as a matter simply of racial rather than religious significance. Blacks were initially brought to America as slaves, and their experience in all its dimensions—

including their religious experience—was decisively shaped by this reality. It cannot be compressed into categories derived from the experience of Protestant dissenters, immigrant Catholics or Jews, or other carriers of "religious diversity." The experience of slavery, and the forms of racial oppression that succeeded it, have also placed African Americans in a distinctive relationship to the exercise of political power in this country, for the history of racial injustice in the United States has generally depended more on public policy than private practice. In the history of American Christianity, the problem of theodicy, of justifying the ways of God to humans, has arisen more acutely with regard to race than at any other point. So too has the problem of finding religious legitimation for the American nation-state. Particularly at the present time, when America's global reach has rendered the ultimate meaning of American national power an urgent question everywhere, it is imperative to reckon with these realities. I have attempted to do so in the following pages.

I have also attempted to place the history of Christianity in the United States in the larger context of the globalization of the Christian religion. All too often, the story of American religion at home has been severed from the story of its history abroad. Narratives that highlight the growing religious diversity of the United States sometimes proceed on the assumption that Christianity is a religion of Europeans and of Americans of European descent, and that the increase in America of persons not of European descent is directly and unambiguously correlated with the growth of religions other than Christianity. The reality is far different and more complicated. Increasingly, around the globe, Christianity finds a growing following among persons of color, and Christians in and from the United States are crucially involved in that process. Domestically, it is important to note that the same global immigration which has fueled growing diversity in American religion generally has also made American Christianity significantly less white than it once was. More than is often acknowledged, the birth of African-American Christianity was a critically important phase in the movement of Christianity (most especially Protestantism) beyond the world of Europeans and European Americans, and black Christians in the United States have worked and hoped for a global Christianity unloosed from its ties to white power. Accordingly, I have paid special attention throughout to the relation of black Christians to the American missionary movement. At the same time, I have traced the way the missionary movement of European Americans has meanwhile proceeded in a close, if sometimes deeply uncomfortable, relationship with the global extension of American power.

Admittedly, in using the term "globalization," I have here for the most part spoken loosely of the way enlarging patterns of migration, transportation, and communication have created tightening networks that tie people everywhere into an increasingly common life, but I have also at points alluded to the special role of the American nation-state in structuring this emerging order. This might be rendered more explicit and precise, so far as it relates to religion, by noting the passage in 1998 of the International Religious Freedom Act, which requires the United States government more actively to promote religious freedom everywhere in the world. If globalization is understood in its more restricted sense to mean the universalization of the standards and practices of a free market capitalist economy, then religious globalization can be taken to mean the universalization of the kind of religious liberty practiced in the United States, i.e., a (theoretically) free market in religion. And just as economic globalization has been variously assessed as, from one point of view, the global extension of policies and practices that serve a universal intent or, from another, as a series of arrangements tailored to the economic self-interest of the United States (and the rest of the developed world), so it might be debated whether the International Religious Freedom Act will prompt the United States to protect religious freedom on a universal basis or simply use its power to protect American Christian missionaries, i.e., to open previously closed markets to the "sale" of American religious "products."

Finally, I want to acknowledge that what follows is, in however miniature and detail-laden form, what is sometimes called—usually with pejorative intent—a "grand narrative." For this I do not apologize. As I have already indicated, I think the history of Christianity in the United States—as the history of American religion more generally—appropriately concerns itself, in a central way, with the relation of religious ideas, institutions, constituencies, and practices to the creation and exercise of political power. Certain dimensions of this complex relationship, in my view, can best be addressed through "grand narratives." I am well aware that, in recent times, there has arisen a rather vigorous genre of writings that take as their point of departure the claim that all such narratives inevitably serve the hegemonic aspirations of one or another religious group and need to be exposed, abandoned, and replaced by more modest and admittedly limited accounts. Much of this work, however, seems to me parasitic on the genre it assaults and would in fact be lost without it. And to the extent a (truly) well-meaning attempt to acknowledge America's "many stories" produces surveys that simply meander though our diverse religious landscape respectfully reporting on one group after another, the results—to me at least—are deeply problematic. Trying to write, in a few pages, a succinct narrative history of American Christianity is not easy, and I certainly have no illusions about having gotten the story "right." But "big pictures" will inevitably be drawn and they are far from inconsequential in how we think about our common life in this country.

Acknowledgments

My primary debt here is to Verlag Walter de Gruyter for permission to publish, in English, David W. Wills, "Vereinigte Staaten von Amerika," *Theologische Realenzyklopädie*, gen. ed. Gerhard Müller (Berlin: Walter de Gruyter, 2002), vol. 34, pp. 593–639. I also wish particularly to thank Dr. Albrecht Döhnert, my main point of contact with the TRE, without whose patience, persistence, and occasional electronic indignation at my slow-moving ways, I might never have completed the original German version of this work. I am deeply appreciative as well for the willingness of Barbara Hanrahan of the University of Notre Dame Press, whose aims and skills as an editor I have long admired, to undertake an English-language publication of this work and for her helpfulness in seeing the project through to its conclusion.

To Richard Crouter of Carleton College, I am indebted for suggesting my name to the editors of the TRE as a potential author of this essay. I thank my longtime friend and collaborator, Albert Raboteau of Princeton University, for encouraging me—in response to my initial reluctance—to accept this assignment, and also for advice and encouragement along the way. My many-talented Amherst colleague, Rhonda Cobham-Sander, kindly clarified certain mysteries in the instructions for the essay that my limited command of German had left obscure. In this enterprise as in many other things, I was advised and assisted by Patricia Holland and Scott Sessions, my ever-reliable coworkers in the Amherst College offices of African-American Religion: A Documentary History Project. I am especially obliged to Scott for his typically resourceful, thoughtful, and painstaking work in helping me put the text in final form. I am also grateful to Craig Dykstra and Jean Smith of the Lilly Endowment, whose patient support of the Documentary History Project has enabled a long process of research and reflection that has left a deep mark on this work.

Eddie Glaude of Princeton University I thank for his early—and characteristically vigorous—encouragement to publish this work in English, as well as for keeping after me about other publishing projects. I am indebted to Laurie Maffly-Kipp of the University of North Carolina at Chapel Hill, another longtime friend and collaborator, not only for giving the text a close and helpful reading, but for organizing a public discussion of this work in the fall of 2003. To Grant Wacker of Duke University, and the many UNC and Duke graduate students who participated in that session, I offer my thanks for their advice and encouragement. The preface that I have added to this work attempts, in response to comments made that night, to clarify and underscore the point of view from which this work is written. I am particularly indebted as well to Quincy Newell, now of the University of Wyoming, for following up on that occasion with specific suggestions concerning Native American material. I regret that the architecture of the original essay has made it impossible for me to adopt more than a couple of them. I am also greatly obliged to John P. Reeder of Brown University for his thoughtful reading of the essay and his helpful recommendations about how to make the text more accessible to a beginning reader.

I do not imagine that this small work will end the needling, which has intermittently arisen over many years from the ranks of "Wills, party of twelve" (and counting), about my apparently culpable failure to produce a "best-seller." But I trust it will somehow find its way into the web of bantering allusion that my loving and beloved family so skillfully weaves.

The dedication names the two immigrants from Scotland whose arrival in the United States with their three daughters in 1923 marks the moment when my ancestors' direct participation in the story of American Christianity is clearly known to begin. So little do such twentieth-century British immigrants figure in the history of American religion that it took me a long time to understand that being the son of an immigrant mother was scarcely an inconsequential part of who I am—and therefore how I think about the United States. I am sure it matters as well that not even the names of my orphaned father's parents have come down to me, though it seems one or the other of them was named Wills and was not an immigrant. Where they may be hidden in the story I tell here, I cannot say. One tale has it that they were southern Methodists, and it is easy for me to imagine such ancestors, immersed in the southern racial realities of slavery and segregation. But it is only a tale.

CHRISTIANITY

IN THE UNITED STATES

Introduction

The history of Christianity in the United States, deeply shaped throughout by an ever-expanding confluence of peoples and the contention and mutual transformation this inevitably brings, may be seen as a central aspect of the ongoing globalization of the Christian religion. Rooted most immediately in the Atlantic world's early history, three centuries in which the peoples of Europe, Africa, and the Americas were brought together in an altogether unprecedented way through a complex process of commerce, conquest, and colonization (of which the British settlement of the North American coast was only one phase), the new American nation-state that emerged from the revolutionary struggle with Great Britain was stamped in its church membership and public ethos predominantly by a British Protestantism rooted in the Reformed tradition. Nevertheless, this British Protestant tradition was itself internally diverse, existed alongside a highly variegated Protestantism of continental European (primarily German) origins, as well as small constituencies of Catholics and Jews, and shared the land with a substantial and mostly enslaved African-descended population and many Native American peoples that were only slightly Christianized during the colonial era. During the nineteenth century and up until the 1920s, American Christianity was rendered increasingly diverse and sometimes bitterly divided. In part, this diversity and division resulted from a multitude of new movements and fresh schisms (above all over the practice of racial slavery) arising among Protestants of British descent and in part from territorial expansion that in Florida, Louisiana, and the Southwest annexed a largely Catholic population. Even more, however, it was the result of a massive immigration that drew from an ever-widening number of European nations and peoples (many of them largely Roman Catholic, some primarily Orthodox) and by the growing conversion to Christianity of African Americans and Native Americans. Immigration also brought increasing numbers of Jews and, in the latter half of this period and primarily in the American West, created a significant Asian minority. During the years from the mid-1920s until the mid-1960s, legal restrictions that sharply curtailed immigration shaped a period in which Christianity in the United States seemed to have achieved greater internal stability within the context of greater cultural consensus. The ongoing proliferation of new Protestant groups was balanced by an increasing emphasis on denominational mergers and ecumenical cooperation and an emerging (though far from universal) consensus acknowledging Protestantism, Catholicism, and Judaism as equally acceptable forms of American religion. After the mid-1960s, however, the patterns of the previous period reasserted themselves. The cultural ferment of the 1960s marked the onset of a severe institutional weakening of the core denominations of the old Protestant mainstream, which less and less were able to define the center of American Christianity. Catholicism in the United States entered into a period of increased public influence, yet also a time of growing internal conflict. The civil rights movement, which won in the mid-1960s an end to the legal enforcement of racial segregation in the southern states, inaugurated a time when African Americans became both more insistent on fair treatment within American society and the Christian churches and more receptive to religions other than Christianity. Above all, a major change in the nation's immigration laws in 1965 reopened the United States to large-scale immigration, which now came at unprecedented levels not only from Latin America and the Caribbean, but also from Africa and Asia. This immigration has meant the increasing presence within America of religious traditions previously not of numerical significance, above all Islam, a fateful reality with which the American churches have only begun to deal. At the same time, it has also meant significantly increasing diversity within the world of American Christianity itself.

It must be emphasized that at no point in this long and complex history has the mere fact of plurality as such, either within American Christianity or in American religion generally, produced in some automatic or uncontested way a normative vision of "pluralism," i.e., some widely shared affirmation of religious diversity or common definition of its acceptable forms. Rather, at every point, normative conceptions of religious plurality, which inevitably embrace some forms of religious belief and practice while excluding others, have been a central point of contention in American Christianity. In the nation's early history, Protestants who had come to accept a degree of doctrinal difference and variation in practice among themselves as acceptable diversity within a shared framework were seldom ready to accept Roman Catholics on the same basis. Twentieth-century Christians who had adjusted to the tripartite pluralism of Catholics, Protestants, and Jews were less sure of the terms on which Islam in America was to be embraced. Meanwhile, throughout American history, there have ever and again been Christian movements that have taken as their point of departure an alleged excess of diversity and individualism, and called for a renewed commitment to common values and communal discipline. Recurrently, in this context, the example of the earliest American Puritans has sometimes been invoked as a model of collective religious aspiration from which subsequent generations have declined. And always there has remained—as there still does—the question of whether any standard of pluralism, religious or otherwise, or any articulation of shared values, is adequate for addressing the deepest and still unresolved question of American life—the legacy of racial slavery, a task to which American Christians have set themselves only episodically.

CHAPTER 1

Colonies in the Atlantic World

Christianity Enters the Early Atlantic World

The history of Christianity in the United States of America is rooted in the prior history of the Atlantic world (which may be thought of, in the most simple terms, as an interrelated set of sustained human interactions mediated by the Atlantic Ocean). Emerging in the fifteenth century with the voyages of exploration, slaving, and trade conducted under Portuguese auspices along the west coast of Africa, the Atlantic world became after Columbus's voyage of 1492 a transatlantic world in which the confluence of African, European, and American Indian peoples provided the basic human background for all other developments. At the outset, Christianity entered the new Atlantic world with a vision defined by Mediterranean precept and practice. The Portuguese initially saw their African enterprise as an extension of their North African battles with Islam, while Columbus assured the Spanish monarchs that the wealth of the New World would enable them to conquer Jerusalem. The institution of slavery, revived in the Latin Christian world of the late Middle Ages and interpreted in close relation to (and in parallel with) just war theory,[1]

---

1. Just war theory, for many centuries the prevailing view in Christian moral reflection on warfare, seeks to establish standards governing both the resort to war (e.g., last resort) and the conduct of war (e.g., noncombatant

was carried into the Atlantic world as a major means for the organization of non-European labor and a primary context in which the evangelization of non-European peoples often proceeded. In lands controlled by the Iberian powers, the church relied heavily on the confraternity as a mechanism for the integration of non-European converts into the Christian world. Though the Portuguese initially took steps to draw Africans into the priesthood, even promoting the ordination of a Kongo prince to the bishopric in 1520, and though recurrent efforts were subsequently made on both sides of the Atlantic to open the clergy to non-Europeans, a racial bar was more often enforced than not. Such barriers profoundly shaped the development of Christianity in the Atlantic world, ensuring that formal religious leadership, like political authority and economic power, long remained almost exclusively in the hands of Europeans.

In its early history, the Christianity of the Atlantic world was entirely Roman Catholic. Already by the late sixteenth century, however, Protestant powers were increasingly intruding on the Portuguese-Spanish monopoly on both sides of the Atlantic, and French Huguenots (Protestants) as well as French Roman Catholics also began to make their presence felt in the Americas. It was an attempt in the 1560s by Huguenots to settle colonies in present-day South Carolina and Florida that prompted Spain to establish its first permanent outpost in what is now the United States, at Saint Augustine, Florida, in 1563. A series of previous Spanish attempts, launched from Spain's colonies in the Caribbean islands beginning in 1513 and including the heroic if ill-fated missionary enterprise of the Dominican Luis Cáncer de Barbastro in 1549, had all failed to secure a lasting base. Meanwhile, a parallel series of expeditions, pressing northward from New Spain, eventually succeeded in establishing an enduring Spanish presence in what is now New Mexico. Santa Fe, organized as a municipality in 1610, became the area's capital. From this base, and later

---

immunity from direct attack). Parallel thinking about slavery sought to establish standards governing both who could be enslaved (e.g., captives taken in a just war) and the treatment of slaves (e.g., the right to marry).

from other outposts stretching from Texas to the Pacific coast of California, Spanish Catholicism put a lasting imprint on the religious life of the American Southwest. Such Spanish successes did not, however, deter France, England, the Netherlands, or even Sweden from establishing colonies in North America in the early seventeenth century. French expeditions had probed the Saint Lawrence River as early as the 1530s and some effort had been made there and elsewhere in Canada to create permanent outposts, but Quebec was founded only in 1608. Here, as in the more or less simultaneous development of a French settlement at Acadia (in contemporary Nova Scotia), both Huguenots and Roman Catholics were involved. The steady erosion of Protestantism's place in the France of Cardinal Richelieu (1585–1642) meant, however, that New France soon became a thoroughly Catholic undertaking, and as such a religious as well as a geopolitical rival to the colonies of British North America. At the same time, a number of French Huguenots from across the Atlantic world, especially after the revocation of the Edict of Nantes in 1685, emigrated to the English colonies, most especially New York and South Carolina, where they did not long sustain a distinctive religious identity, but instead quickly became assimilated by the prevailing English Protestantism.

The first enduring English settlement in North America was established at Jamestown, Virginia, in 1607. Here too, the founding of a permanent outpost occurred only after a series of failures. It was quickly followed, however, by other successes. In 1620, the Pilgrims, attempting to reach Virginia, landed instead in what is now Massachusetts in New England and established a settlement at Plymouth. Within a decade, the more populous and influential Massachusetts Bay colony, dominated by a Puritanism that would long set the tone for Christianity in New England, had also been launched, with its capital at Boston.[2] The Dutch meanwhile had established a presence

---

2. The much-disputed term "Puritanism" refers to a broad, loose, internally diverse, and changing movement, originating in late sixteenth-century England and lasting for a century or so, which sought in various ways to reduce

along the Connecticut, Hudson, and Delaware Rivers, founding in the mid-1620s the colony of New Netherlands. No more than Sweden was able in the long term to hold the small colony it planted along the Delaware River in 1638, however, were the Dutch able to retain control of New Netherlands. The colony fell to the English in 1664, with its core area renamed New York. Nevertheless, the Dutch period set an enduring stamp on the area, as much perhaps in the commercial cosmopolitanism of New Amsterdam as in the enduring influence of Dutch Protestantism. Beyond this area of Dutch settlement, moreover, Dutch influence in the Atlantic world more generally also touched the life of the English colonies in diverse and complicated ways—ranging from the refuge provided to the Pilgrims when they first fled England and the influence of Dutch theologians on the New England Puritans to the fact that the first African slaves known to have been sold in Virginia were brought there by a Dutch slaver in 1619.

It is a fact of decisive significance that most of the thirteen continental colonies of British North America that eventually formed the

---

the nation's lingering Catholic legacy and bring English religious—and public— life into closer conformity with strict Protestant standards, most often those of the Reformed (Calvinist) branch of the European Reformation. Generally, Puritans affirmed the Calvinist belief that those who would be saved, the "elect," had been predestined by God for salvation before the creation of the world. They disagreed among themselves about the proper way of organizing the church. Some found the episcopal organization of the Church of England acceptable, others (Presbyterians) called for the replacement of bishops and archbishops with regional and national assemblies, still others (Congregationalists) were to varying degrees opposed to all forms of ecclesiastical authority beyond the local congregation. Baptists generally began from Congregational premises and added the provision that only those sufficiently adult to make a responsible choice could become full, i.e., baptized, members of a church. Numerous other views and smaller groups eventually emerged on the Puritan "left-wing." The Pilgrims were "Separatists," i.e., Congregationalists who were attempting to establish true churches among themselves without waiting for the reform of the Church of England generally. The Puritans of the Massachusetts Bay and Connecticut colonies remained much more concerned with a broad agenda of religious and political reform.

United States were founded in the decades when British Christianity was convulsed by the struggles centering around the Puritan Revolution in England (1640–1660). The ever-widening spectrum of groups which this bitterly contested struggle produced were nearly all exported, at one time or another, to the North American colonies, where they enjoyed highly varied histories. Some were able to secure dominance in particular colonies and even in some cases to make their version of Christianity the politically established faith—though everywhere the presence of growing diversity and, after 1689, the English Act of Toleration, rendered compromises necessary. English Catholics, eager for a shelter in the Protestant storm, established the colony of Maryland in 1634, where they of necessity practiced a religious toleration that eventually undermined Catholic control. By the end of the century, the colony had an Anglican (i.e., Church of England) establishment. The Church of England, as established in early Virginia, had a strong Puritan cast, but this was less true of the Anglicanism that eventually enjoyed state support in Maryland and further south in the colonies of North Carolina and South Carolina, founded in the 1660s. Elsewhere, Anglicans were a minority. Presbyterians, both English and Scottish, who did not take distinct and enduring organizational form in North America until the early eighteenth century, became strongest in New Jersey and the adjacent colonies (and later in the eighteenth century in the back country of the southern colonies as well), but they nowhere controlled the religious life of a new colony. Their closest theological and ecclesiastical kin, meanwhile, the "nonseparating" Congregationalists, held a control of the Massachusetts and Connecticut colonies so complete that Congregational churches there enjoyed state privileges into the early nineteenth century, well after such establishments had been ended elsewhere. Such Congregationalists also played a prominent role in the early history of that part of the present-day state of New Jersey known as East Jersey, where they began to settle in the 1660s. The separatist Congregationalists initially controlled the Plymouth colony, but this slow-growing community was absorbed by the Massachusetts Bay colony in 1691. Baptists appeared as early as the 1630s, under the leadership of Roger Williams (1603/4–1683) in Providence, but they shared the evolving colony of Rhode Island (chartered only in 1663) with Separatists, Quakers, and other religious radicals in flight from the Puritan colonies. The number of Baptists (who were ever more theologically diverse and varied in their forms of church organization) was steadily increased both by immigration, mostly from England, and by periodic waves of conversion from other Protestant groups. Eventually they spread throughout colonial British America, yet in the colonial period they remained everywhere a minority. Markedly different was the experience of the Society of Friends. Initially in West Jersey, which took shape in the 1670s, and then more notably in Pennsylvania (1681), Quakers were able to control new colonies, giving them—particularly in the case of the latter—a distinctive character they long retained even after immigration had undermined the Quaker majority. Significant numbers of Quakers were also to be found in other colonies, especially in the upper South.

It is important to recall, as it often has not been by historians of North American religion, that the British settlement of North America took place not only against the backdrop of the Puritan Revolution and its transformation of British religious life, but also in relation to the creation of a British Atlantic-world empire in which the practice of racial slavery—and therefore the presence of a multitude of Africans—was an essential constitutive reality. In 1660, the combined population of England's two largest North American colonies, Virginia and Massachusetts, was less than that of England's lucrative sugar-planting slave-labor island colony of Barbados. A century later in 1760, counting everything from Nova Scotia to the Leeward Islands, as well as the thirteen North American colonies that created the United States, the population of Britain's Atlantic empire was one-third African. Particularly with regard to the history of the globalization of Christianity, this is a fact of first importance. In writing the history of the missionary movements through which Protestantism contributed to the creation of world Christianity, historians sometimes begin, so far as the English-speaking world is concerned, with the movement that emerged in England at the end of the eighteenth century. By this time, however, the encounter of Protestants with non-European peoples in the Atlantic world was already well under way, and should be reckoned as the prehistory of the later missionary movement. The Church of England assigned responsibility for its overseas colonies to the bishop of London, and Henry Compton (1632–1713), who held this position from 1675–1713, was obliged to address, however tentatively, the question of how to deal, so far as religion was concerned, with both the Native Americans and the very substantial African-born or African-descended slave population of Britain's Atlantic empire. The efforts along these lines by the Society for the Propagation of the Gospel in Foreign Parts, established by the Church of England in 1701, though no doubt largely ineffective, were nonetheless significant and prophetic.

Three Enduring Themes

In summarizing the enduring influence of the colonial period on the subsequent religious history of the United States, it is useful to group the North American colonies into three larger regions, each of which may be seen to exemplify a central theme. Each of these themes— religious and cultural diversity (Middle Colonies), the quest for a holy commonwealth (New England), and the encounter of black and white (the South)—is foundational for later developments and may indeed be traced through the entirety of American religious history, right down to the present time.

The Middle Colonies of New York, New Jersey, Pennsylvania, and Delaware are the area in which later American patterns of ethnic and cultural diversity and religious liberty are most anticipated. It has long been debated whether early movements toward religious liberty in the American colonies are to be seen as a pragmatic adaptation by the indifferent or a principled innovation by the devout. In the Middle Colonies one can see both patterns exemplified, in the matter-of-fact acceptance of diversity in New York and in the more idealistic Quaker commitment to toleration in Pennsylvania. In any case, none of the Middle Colonies was dominated by an effective religious establishment and everywhere there was considerable variety. Most notably, Pennsylvania in the eighteenth century welcomed a steadily growing immigration of Germans, who came to constitute the largest of the continental European groups in the British North American colonies. Like the English who came to North America during the era of the Puritan Revolution, they brought with them the burgeoning religious diversity of their homeland, most particularly of the Rhineland provinces from which many of them came. The spectrum ranged from Lutherans and Reformed through such pietist groups as the Church of the Brethren (Dunkers) and the Renewed Church of the United Brethren (Moravians) to the Mennonites. For a time, the radically pietistic Ephrata Community served as a cultural focal point for Pennsylvania Germans generally.[3]

Patterns in New England, which in the colonial period included Massachusetts, Connecticut, New Hampshire, and Rhode Island, were notably different. Although Rhode Island was one of the most important sites, along with Pennsylvania, of an early movement toward the principled institutionalization of religious liberty, the main thrust of New England Puritanism was toward the creation of a "holy commonwealth." The Puritan leaders of the Massachusetts Bay and Connecticut colonies did not come to the New World to institute a general religious liberty, but to establish a social and ecclesiastical order fully exemplifying their own distinctive ideas, which they hoped would guide the ongoing course of the Reformation in Britain and the European continent. Their ideas included an unusual

---

3. The use of the term "Pietism" is far-ranging and contested. Here it refers to a broad movement, emerging in continental Protestantism in the late seventeenth century and extending into the following century, which placed particular emphasis on inward piety, personal holiness, and works of charity. Like Puritanism, with which it overlapped, Pietism produced over time a wide variety of groups, some adhering closely to the doctrines and practices of the Lutheran and Reformed churches of Europe, and others adopting highly distinctive teachings, practices, and forms of organization.

and seemingly unstable blend of churchly beliefs about the importance of state-supported religious uniformity and inclusiveness with
a sectarian commitment to a congregational church polity, a tension
vividly evident in their attempt simultaneously to practice infant
baptism while restricting the Lord's Supper to carefully scrutinized
"visible saints." As evident in the early cases of Roger Williams and
Anne Hutchinson (1591–1643) and her "Antinomian" followers, New
England Puritanism consistently generated sectarian dissenters from
within. Nevertheless, the enduring legacy of the Puritan tradition in
America has been most evident in recurrent religiously informed
efforts to define and achieve some exemplary state of public morality
and /or social justice, a goal understood as the nation's collective religious destiny. Again and again, critics of American life troubled by a
seeming excess of competitive individualism, moral laxity, and social injustice have invoked the spirit if not the words of the Massachusetts Bay colony's first governor, John Winthrop (1588–1643),
who summoned his fellow colonists to devote themselves not to private gain but to the shared work of building a holy "city upon a
hill" for the whole world to see. New England Puritanism, which included among its founders a cadre of university-educated clergy un-
paralleled in the early history of the Middle Colonies and the South,
also profoundly shaped the history of theology in America, in part
through its early influence in American higher education, evident in
the founding in 1636 and 1701 respectively of the colleges that eventually became Harvard University and Yale University.

The religious history of the southern colonies—Virginia, Maryland, North Carolina, South Carolina, and eventually (settled first
in 1733) Georgia—has sometimes been interpreted as simply a variation on the story of the more northern colonies. Certainly, the Puritan impulse was evident in the southern colonies, and they contained
as well significant ethnic and religious diversity, particularly in the
back country during the eighteenth century. Nevertheless, the dominant feature of southern religious life was the division of the population along racial lines, with the blacks and whites confronting one
another across a vast gulf constituted on the one side by a marked

divergence of cultural inheritance and religious practice and on the other by the practice of racial slavery. Europeans brought with them to the Americas, as recent scholarship has been at pains to emphasize, not only various forms of Christian (and to a small degree Jewish) beliefs and practices, but also a wide range of occult and "magical" ideas and techniques. Such traditions offered a point of contact with African (as well as Native American) ways of understanding and managing spiritual power, but it was initially quite otherwise with the various forms of European Christianity, which in the early colonial period made little headway in attracting black converts. Whether, how, and to what extent Africans were able to sustain their inherited religious traditions in the American environment remains a matter of scholarly dispute, but the prevailing view is that they preserved at the very least some traditional beliefs and practices, albeit modified no doubt by the rigors of slavery, their own ethnic diversity, and above all the uprooting of the kinship structures with which the religions of Africa are so closely interwoven. The African slave population also included some Muslims, though Islamic practice was hard to sustain under the conditions of American slavery, and their presence remains an elusive one in the historical record. Meanwhile, the churches continued the long-prevailing Christian pattern of accepting the institution of slavery, but appealing—in this case not usually very energetically—for its moral regulation. Fears that baptizing slaves would require their emancipation, though repeatedly addressed by colonial and church authorities—most notably in the bishop of London's 1727 statement that Christianity did not free converts from the duties of their social station—persisted and fueled planter resistance to missionary efforts among their slaves. Though Africans were less numerous outside the South (where they were in some times and places a majority of the population) and though slavery was much less important economically in most of the Middle Colonies and New England, the black presence and racial slavery were everywhere part of the social world in which American Christianity took shape.

The Transforming Influence of the Enlightenment and
the Evangelical Revivals

Each of these foundational motifs—growing religious and cultural diversity, the Puritan quest for a holy commonwealth, and the encounter of blacks and whites in the context of racial slavery—was transformed during the later colonial period not only by a range of economic, social, and political developments, but also by the ethos of the Enlightenment and the emergence of evangelicalism. These two transatlantic movements, each in its own way and sometimes only haltingly and indirectly, advanced the practice of religious liberty, redefined Puritan notions of collective purpose and the common good, and stimulated both the critique of slavery and the conversion of African Americans. The relative importance of each movement, in shaping the process of change out of which the American Revolution eventually emerged, has been much debated. The claim that the United States is an Enlightenment nation everywhere stamped by the ideas of John Locke (1632–1704)—and the Whig tradition generally—has been met with the counterclaim that the revolutionary spirit was forged in the fires of the evangelical Great Awakening of the 1730s and 1740s (fires set ablaze above all by the Anglican evangelist George Whitefield [1714–1770]), the first major cultural event binding together all the colonies of British America. To this assertion it has in turn been replied in recent years that the very concept of the "Great Awakening" is a nineteenth-century invention that retrospectively confused an intense revival in New England with more superficial developments elsewhere, especially in the South. Meanwhile, the notion that the Enlightenment is to be understood, so far as religion is concerned, primarily with a rationalistic deism or skepticism has itself been challenged.

With regard to the movement toward increased toleration and the institutionalization of religious liberty, it is clear that the decisive theoretical and political leadership was provided by the deistically inclined Thomas Jefferson (1743–1826; president, 1801–1809) and

James Madison (1751–1836; president, 1809–1817).[4] The Virginia Act for Religious Freedom, drafted by Jefferson and adopted through Madison's leadership in 1786, declared freedom of religious belief a natural right and ended state support for all religious bodies. It set the precedent for the treatment of religion under the new federal constitution. The First Amendment (ratified in 1791) required the Congress of the United States to "make no law respecting an establishment of religion, or prohibiting the free exercise thereof." This movement toward religious liberty drew support as well from dissenting groups throughout the colonies, most especially the Baptists, a widespread and growing constituency by the end of the eighteenth century. Nevertheless, it was by no means universally embraced, even by the evangelicals.[5] Their growing spirit of toleration rested on a willingness to overlook (at least some) doctrinal differences among those who shared a broad orthodoxy and a vital piety, but they were often not committed to the elimination of all state support for the Protestant churches. Jefferson and Madison's opponents in Virginia were not die-hard defenders of the Anglican (now Episcopal) state church, but proponents of a more inclusive Protestant establishment, a plan that had considerable report in several of the other states

---

4. Deism affirmed a God who created the world, endowed it with a moral order accessible to human reason, and administers a system of rewards and punishments, but rejected the claims of Christianity (and other religions) to know by special revelation a considerable body of additional doctrines and precepts required for right thinking and living.

5. The term "Evangelicalism," like Puritanism and Pietism, designates a complex, changing, and much-debated phenomenon. A reform movement emerging in English-speaking Protestantism in the middle decades of the eighteenth century, evangelicalism is best known for drawing a sharp contrast between those Christians who had been truly "born again" and those who had not. Like Puritanism and Pietism, to which it was closely related, Evangelicalism spawned a spectrum of leaders and groups, some of whom were more radically innovative than others. Common themes were the importance of a conversion experience, the pursuit of holy living, and a concern to purify the churches of their "worldliness."

during the Revolutionary and early national eras. Above all in New England, neither the Virginia example nor the federal constitution ended public support for the traditionally established churches. Yet so far as long-term implications for the global history of Christianity are concerned, it was the more or less willing adjustment that the American churches eventually made to the practice of religious liberty that was decisive for later developments.

As is demonstrated by the later ability of Massachusetts, Connecticut, and New Hampshire to hold out against this trend and to sustain into the early nineteenth century, in however modified a form, public support for the Congregational churches, the most powerful Christians in these states were tenaciously committed to the idea of a religiously grounded public order. Nevertheless, Puritan New England had never lacked internal divisions (something increasingly stressed by recent scholarship), and the varied currents of the Enlightenment and evangelicalism compounded this. The theological center of gravity in seventeenth-century New England lay in a Calvinist orthodoxy deeply infused with the scholastic tradition. In the eighteenth century, the moralizing, Arminian currents of the moderate Enlightenment and the experiential emphasis of evangelicalism widened the already existing divisions between the intellectualist and voluntarist sides of the New England Puritan tradition, as became clearly visible in the Awakening-era contention between Charles Chauncy (1705–1787) and Jonathan Edwards (1703–1758). In Jonathan Edwards, New England's Puritan tradition produced a theologian of the first order, whose deep immersion in the religious life of his own locality should not obscure his wide-ranging awareness of the intellectual currents of the Atlantic world more generally. As much as the genial deism of Benjamin Franklin (1706–1790), Edwards's distinctive rendering of evangelical Calvinism was closely attuned to contemporary currents in European thought, most especially with respect to growing emphasis on the place of the affections in the moral life. Edwards's more provincial heirs, most notably Samuel Hopkins (1721–1803) and Joseph Bellamy (1719–1790), carried forward this "New Divinity," a movement which sustained some creativity and an important place in New England theology well into the nineteenth century.

More generally, Edwards's speculations that the intense revivals of his day signaled the coming of the millennium—beginning in New England—have sometimes been seen as anticipating and in part fostering the millennialism of the Revolutionary era, when the birth of the new nation was seen as the beginning of a new age.[6] Revolutionary optimism also drew, however, on the progressive views of history associated with the Enlightenment, and not all the millennialism of the period was focused on political events. The Shakers, immigrants from England where they had been influenced by the traditions of the French Prophets, arrived in New York in 1774. For them, the New Age was signaled by Christ's second appearance on earth, in the person of Ann Lee (1736–1784). Exceptional in many particulars, most obviously perhaps in their practice of celibacy, they nevertheless indicated the growing tendency of radical evangelicalism to insist on a religious leadership role for women. Meanwhile, the general political optimism of the Revolutionary period was shadowed by the more somber ethos of classical Republicanism, with its warning that the new political order could be secured only by the enduring virtue of its citizens, and by orthodox Protestant anxieties about the inroads of deism and skepticism.

The coordinate influences of rationalistic moralism and evangelical fervor are also evident in the period's invigorated movement to end slavery. In the pre-Revolutionary period, the Quakers were the only major Christian group to challenge the institution directly, but antislavery voices now became numerous and louder among a range of other groups as well, including Congregationalists, Presbyterians, Baptists, and Methodists (who appeared in British North

---

6. Christians had generally interpreted the Bible to teach that human history would culminate in a "millennium," i.e., a thousand-year period, in which Christ would reign on earth. Millennialism refers to the belief that this thousand years of peace and justice was about to begin or had already done so.

America in the 1770s and increased in number with great rapidity). The transatlantic slave trade was restricted or eliminated by most of the new states, and provision was made in the federal constitution that Congress could after twenty years outlaw the practice generally (which it did). The northern states also took steps to end slavery itself, though in most cases the process of emancipation proceeded only very gradually, sometimes taking decades fully to complete. In the southern states, slavery remained both fully legal and deeply entrenched. Meanwhile, evangelical efforts to convert slaves and free blacks to Christianity proceeded with growing if still modest success. Already in the awakenings of the 1730s and 1740s, beginning with the Moravians in the Virgin Islands, various evangelical groups had commenced new missionary efforts among the slaves. In British North America, the remarkable Anglican evangelist George Whitefield greatly stimulated this enterprise, not only by himself winning black converts during his much-publicized preaching tours, but also by inspiring many other evangelicals who carried such work forward in the middle decades of the eighteenth century. During the Revolutionary era—and for long thereafter—the greatest success was achieved by the Baptists and Methodists. The evangelicals' success among African Americans may in part have rested on the resonance between their emphasis on an intensely felt, publicly expressed piety and African traditions of trance and possession, but it also sprang— especially with the Baptists and Methodists—from their willingness to employ black exhorters and preachers, some of whom organized black congregations and some of whom were eventually ordained. This marked a significant if still very limited opening in the wall that had separated persons of color from formally acknowledged leadership in the Christian churches of the Atlantic world.

From the standpoint of American churches' place in the globalization of Christianity, note must also be taken of an emerging interest in using freed slaves from America to inaugurate missionary work in Africa. In 1774, under the leadership of Samuel Hopkins, an effort was begun to recruit and educate a few black Christians for this purpose. Disrupted by the upheavals of the Revolutionary War, the effort failed, but it set a precedent not only for later efforts to plant colonies of Christian blacks in Africa, but also for the American foreign missions movement more generally. Even during this period, moreover, some African-American Christians did succeed in spreading their own faith more widely in the Atlantic world. A cadre of early black preachers (most notably the ex-slave Baptists David George [1742–1810] and George Liele [1752–1825]), who found the freedom of blacks better served by the British than by the Americans and left with other Loyalists when the British withdrew, planted black congregations in such places as Jamaica, Nova Scotia, and eventually in Sierra Leone. Notable too is the career of John Marrant (1755–1791), a South Carolina black who was ordained in 1786 in England by the Countess of Huntington's Connection and preached for a time in Nova Scotia. Some of his followers eventually established that church too in Sierra Leone.

CHAPTER 2

A Continental Nation-State

Political and Religious Background

The history of Christianity in the period from the drafting of the constitution (1787) until the First World War occurs within the context of a developing nation-state transforming itself from a politically insecure series of settlements located primarily along the Atlantic coast into a transcontinental world power stretching from the Atlantic to the Pacific. Inevitably, Christian groups were deeply preoccupied with developing and managing institutional structures suited to an ever-expanding space that came eventually to include all of North America lying between the present borders of Canada and Mexico—as well as Hawaii, Alaska, Puerto Rico, and the Virgin Islands. With equal inevitability, they were caught up as well in the social and political controversies surrounding this expansion, most notably in the great debate over the expansion of slavery into newly acquired territories, which culminated in the bloody Civil War of 1861–1865. Meanwhile, the population of this growing nation-state was profoundly transformed not only by the huge natural increase of the colonial population, but also by the conquest of new peoples, mostly Indian, and above all by a massive and increasingly diverse immigration, which deeply affected the profile of American Christianity during this period. The three enduring problematics inherited from the Atlantic-world era—managing religious and cultural diversity, striving for a holy commonwealth, and confronting the gap between blacks and whites—all persisted into the continental period, where they took new and changing forms. At the same time, the interest of Christians in the United States in overseas missions, first evident in the faltering effort to send black Christians to Africa, gradually grew in scope during this period, matching at its end the nascent international reach of the American nation-state.

The task of managing religious diversity, above all by defining some normative concept of acceptable religious pluralism, was complicated during this period by a vast enlargement of Christian groups (as well as a smaller but nonetheless significant increase in the range of religious traditions outside Christianity). The enlarging of religious diversity was rooted to a large extent in the changing population, most especially in the flood of European immigrants. The aggregate numbers are staggering. The total volume of immigration rose from around 150,000 for the decade of the 1820s to a peak of about 8,750,000 for the first decade of the twentieth century. The 1850s, when over two and a half million immigrants came, was the decade in which the ratio of immigrants to the preexisting nonimmigrant population stood at its highest. The importation of enslaved Africans, such a prominent feature of the prior era, became illegal in 1808 and occurred only clandestinely and in smaller number, a change which eventually led to a decline in the persistence of traditional African religious practices and the seeming disappearance of Islam among blacks. At the same time, however, immigration from Asia, most importantly but not only from China and Japan, gradually introduced into the United States, albeit on a very small scale, the practice of such traditions as Hinduism, Buddhism, and Confucianism, while Middle Eastern immigrants, though in this era largely Christian, also included small numbers of Muslims. Westward expansion brought many additional Native American peoples within the borders of the United States, although, largely confined to reservations, they were long treated as aliens. Among the Europeans, English-speaking immigrants still constituted the largest single language group, but they were sharply divided between English, Scottish, and

Scotch-Irish Protestants and Irish Roman Catholics. Germans, who (as they had been in the colonial era) constituted the second largest language group, were even more diverse religiously, including not only Protestants and Catholics, but also a significant number of Jews. Generally, other language groups (the Italians made up the largest among them) were relatively more homogenous religiously, yet they were in turn typically more different religiously from the older European-American population. The eastern European immigrants of the latter decades of this period also included a significant minority of Orthodox Christians. Taken together, European immigration in this period redrew the map of American religious diversity. Protestantism in the United States retained the marks of its primarily British origins, but to the strong German minority was added, especially in the Middle West, a range of Scandinavian groups, largely Lutheran. Jews, internally divided—sometimes very sharply—among a small body of descendants of the mostly Sephardic population of the Atlantic-world era and much larger groups of Germans and eastern Europeans, became a visible and influential body of believers standing outside the prevailing Christianity. The single largest change, however, was probably the creation of a very sizable and internally diverse population of Roman Catholics.

Roman Catholicism

Already by the mid-nineteenth century, though still far outnumbered by Protestants as a whole, Roman Catholics were the single largest church in the United States, exceeding in number even the largest of the individual Protestant denominations. Although in the early decades of this period Catholic leadership was predominantly Anglo-American and French (the Sulpicians played a particularly important role), the Irish may already have constituted a majority of the laity. The four and a half million immigrants from Ireland who came to the United States between 1820 and 1920 made the Irish presence in the American Catholic church decisive at every level, especially in the antebellum period and enduringly in the states along the eastern seaboard. Having largely abandoned Gaelic in Ireland, the English-speaking Irish were well positioned to assume Catholic leadership in the United States. They not only came to dominate the leadership of the church, they also stamped it with their own form of piety, which was not so much traditionally Irish as it was an expression of nineteenth-century Roman reforms. Large numbers of German Catholics, coming throughout the same period, however, challenged the Irish hegemony, especially in the Middle West. Bavarian Benedictines established a number of important monasteries, most notably St. John's Abbey in Minnesota, which in the next century would play an important role in the liturgical reforms achieved at the Second Vatican Council. German and Irish Catholics differed with increasing regularity as the century advanced, contending over a wide range of issues, including the embrace of the temperance movement by many Irish bishops and the alleged inability of Irish priests effectively to minister to German Catholics. In the early 1890s, a group of German Catholics attempted unsuccessfully to persuade the Vatican to reorganize the Roman Catholic Church in America into parallel ethnic institutions. Meanwhile, the changing sources of immigration in the late nineteenth and early twentieth centuries had created other sizable ethnic constituencies, of which the Italian and Polish were the largest and most important. They differed not only from the Irish and the Germans, but also one another, the Italians being devoutly attached to a familial and communal but somewhat anti-institutional popular piety, while the Poles were generally more parish-oriented and institutionally loyal, a difference sometimes attributed to the contrasting relations of nationalism and Catholicism in Italy and Poland. The continental expansion of the United States meanwhile had added to the ethnic mix of American Catholicism constituencies developed long before by the French (and Spanish) in Louisiana and the Spanish in Florida and the Southwest. Black Catholics, clustered in the antebellum period in such centers of Catholic slaveholding as Maryland, Kentucky, and Louisiana, abandoned the church in significant numbers with the end of slavery in the 1860s. The work of the Mill Hill (Josephite) Fathers, beginning in the early 1870s, and the formation by Katherine Drexel (1858–1955) of the Society of the Blessed Sacrament for Indians and Colored People in 1891 marked an attempt to reverse this trend, even as the Colored Catholic Congresses organized by Daniel Rudd (1854–1932) in the late 1880s and early 1890s revealed the emergence of a self-conscious black Catholic minority. Apart from the special case of the mulatto Healy brothers, ordained abroad in the 1850s and 1860s and advanced to the presidency of Georgetown College (Francis Patrick Healy [1834–1910], 1874) and the episcopacy (James Augustine Healy [1830–1900], 1875), no African Americans were ordained to the priesthood until 1886, and few in the decades immediately after that.

Varied Forms of Evangelical Protestantism

Even as Roman Catholicism established itself as the largest religious minority in a predominantly Protestant country, the world of American Protestantism itself became ever more diverse and divided, in part through immigration, but even more through recurrent waves of innovation and controversy that swept through the native-born Protestant population. Recent scholarship has placed increased emphasis on how deeply American Christianity was reshaped in the early national period by an explosion of popular movements informed in part by the democratic ethos associated with Jeffersonian and Jacksonian political movements, but also by ongoing traditions of millennialism and of occult practice. Though highly varied in their theological emphases, the prevailing (though by no means universal) tendency among such groups was to move steadily away from the Reformed orthodoxy so strong in the pre-Revolutionary era. In the 1790s and the first decade of the nineteenth century, a series of movements arose rejecting all existing denominations as human inventions, calling for a return to the New Testament, and adopting the simple name "Christian." The larger of these coalesced in 1832 and, led by Alexander Campbell (1788–1866), the Disciples of Christ became a major force in the border South and the Ohio Valley. The Universalists, whose beginnings lay in the 1770s, expanded in the early 1800s under the leadership of Hosea Ballou (1771–1852). Both groups combined a revivalistic evangelical ethos with a strong streak of religious rationalism. In the revivalistic excitement of the "Second Great Awakening" of the early 1800s, another group rooted in the Revolutionary period, the United Society of Believers in Christ's Second Coming (the Shakers) won increased adherents in both New England and the trans-Appalachian West. Their celibate, quasi-monastic settlements, with both male and female leadership, inspired communal experiments by a diverse range of other groups and underscored the growing influence of women in evangelical circles generally, even as their adoption in the 1830s of certain spiritualistic practices anticipated the wider Spiritualist movement triggered in the late 1840s by the Fox sisters. Out of this ferment there also emerged the Church of Jesus Christ of Latter-Day Saints (the Mormons), which some recent scholarship regards not as a Christian movement but as a new religion. Joseph Smith (1805–1844), who claimed in the mid-1820s to have been shown golden plates by the angel Moroni and helped to read them by a special seer stone, published the Book of Mormon in 1830. His growing body of followers established colonies in the West, where increasing conflict with their neighbors led to Smith's lynching, at Nauvoo, Illinois, in 1844. The bulk of his followers set out in the late 1840s, under Brigham Young (1801–1877), for modern Utah, where they sought to establish a holy commonwealth—a patriarchal new Israel where plural marriage became a widespread practice. Meanwhile, William Miller (1782–1849) gathered a sizable following with his predictions of Christ's imminent second advent in 1843 or 1844, and even after the "Great Disappointment" a core constituency remained, which—after increased interaction with Seventh-Day Baptists—led to the formal organization of what eventually became known as the Seventh-Day Adventists. Under the leadership of Ellen G. (née Harmon) White (1827–1915), this group developed a strong and distinctive emphasis on diet and health.

It was none of these groups, however, who won the largest following during the early national period or secured for themselves an enduring place at the numerical center of gravity in American Protestant life. In the religious free market of the nineteenth-century United States, this success was won by the Baptists and the Methodists. In spite of their contrasting organizational styles—one very localistic, the other quite centralized—these two movements, rejecting older traditions of a university-educated clergy, shared a common ability to deploy a veritable army of preachers and exhorters, whose down-to-earth evangelical message was widely accessible to all social ranks. At the same time, compared to such groups as the Shakers, Mormons, or Adventists, their varied theological emphases remained broadly consonant with the Reformed theology of the Presbyterians and Congregationalists, who in turn tended during this period to place increased doctrinal stress on human agency and to adopt some of the revivalistic practices pioneered by the more "popular" groups, as is evident in the life and thought of Nathaniel William Taylor (1786–1858), Lyman Beecher (1775–1863), and Charles Finney (1792–1875). This allowed the Baptists and Methodists to become over time largely "respectable" and to join Congregationalists, Presbyterians, and Episcopalians in an informal "Protestant establishment." Eventually the Disciples of Christ shared in this status as well. Yet even as these groups converged over the nineteenth century into a "Protestant mainstream," deeper and broader than any of its sectarian tributaries, this current flowed forward amidst much turbulence and with fresh divisions. In the early nineteenth century, some of these centered on doctrine or church practice, as in the Methodist disputes over lay participation in governance that led to the founding of the Methodist Protestant Church in 1830, or in Baptist disputes between groups which supported mission societies and those that did not. By midcentury, however, the deepest and most-enduring divisions were rooted in the encounter of blacks and whites under the shadow of slavery.

The Slavery Question

The expectation that slavery was doomed to extinction, common in the Revolutionary era and its immediate aftermath, faded as plantation agriculture spread westward from its southeastern base. With the admission of Missouri as a new slave state in 1820, the struggle to plant the institution in the trans-Mississippi West had begun, intensifying after the United States' conquest of new territories in its war with Mexico in 1845–1846. The major Protestant churches were generally unable either to achieve a stable moral consensus on the institution or effectively to suppress the contention it entailed. Southern Protestants became increasingly insistent on the biblical and moral legitimacy of slaveholding. Northern Protestant opinion was more divided. The radical abolitionist movement that emerged in the 1830s (out of the broad ferment of evangelical radicalism) commanded only a limited following, especially at the outset, yet in the long run it prevented wholesale capitulation to pro-slavery opinion. The largest and most influential Protestant churches were fractured well before a confederacy of southern states made an armed effort to divide the country in 1861. The Presbyterian division of 1837 into New School and Old School bodies involved a number of doctrinal and ecclesiastical issues, but the legitimacy of slavery was an undercurrent. The Old School's most eminent theologian, Charles Hodge (1797–1878) of Princeton Theological Seminary, firmly resisted all efforts to insist that slaveholding was necessarily incompatible with Christianity. The secession of the Methodist Episcopal Church, South from the Methodist Episcopal Church in 1844 and the creation of the Southern Baptist Convention in 1845 were explicitly about northern efforts to enforce restrictions on slaveholders serving, respectively, as bishops and foreign missionaries. During the Civil War, Presbyterians, Methodists, and Baptists on each side of the battle lines invoked the same God on their behalf, each convinced that the future of a social order permeated by evangelical Protestantism would be deeply imperilled by the triumph of the other. Northern and Southern Methodists were not reunited until 1939, nor Presbyterians until the 1970s, while Baptists have never reunited.

African-American Christianity

Meanwhile, evangelical Protestantism began during this period, especially after 1830, to make very substantial gains among African Americans, both slave and free. The black Christianity that developed, however, was distinctive in some of its practices, independent in its view of the American experiment, and sometimes deeply alienated from the white Protestants who had initially promoted it. Already in the early nineteenth century, some African-American Methodists, who had begun organizing separate congregations as early as the 1790s, broke entirely away from the Methodist Episcopal Church, forming completely independent denominations. The most notable of these were the African Methodist Episcopal Church (1816), centered in Philadelphia and Baltimore and led by Richard Allen (1760–1831), and the African Methodist Episcopal Zion Church (the early 1820s) which was centered in New York. The first of these, the AME Church, was the preeminent organization in black America generally during the nineteenth century. Its greatest midcentury leader, Daniel Alexander Payne (1811–1893), a one-time schoolteacher strongly committed to raising the educational level of the church's life, was a highly effective institution builder, but aroused considerable resistance when he sought to suppress such African-derived religious practices as the "ring shout." During the aftermath of the Civil War, a third major black denomination, the Colored Methodist Episcopal Church (later the Christian Methodist Episcopal Church) was organized in the South among ex-slaves. Though working as early as the 1830s through regional associations and conventions, black Baptists did not achieve an enduring denominational organization until the creation of the National Baptist Convention in 1895. A schism in this body in 1915 produced two similarly named churches, the larger National Baptist Convention of the U.S.A., Incorporated, and the National Baptist Convention of America. At the end of the period, these five denominations constituted a kind of black Protestant establishment. Meanwhile, African Americans were also to be found in many predominantly white Protestant churches, usually as a small minority, though in the case of the Methodist Episcopal Church, as a very large constituency.

Though the black denominations as independent bodies were pioneered in the towns and cities of the northern and upper South states, the vast majority of African Americans throughout this period lived in the rural South. During the latter decades of the slavery era, such figures as Charles Colcock Jones (1804–1863) among the Presbyterians and William Capers (1804–1863) among the Methodists successfully promoted systematic "plantation missions," attempts to Christianize African Americans (sometimes termed "Africa at home") that were conscious parallels to the work of foreign missionaries. The most vigorous development of African-American Protestantism occurred, however, not under the watchful eye of such clergy, who were part of the slave regime, but in private meetings presided over by the slaves themselves. From such meetings, the black spirituals emerged. While many American Protestants identified their country as a New Israel in the Promised Land, the slaves sang of God's people in Egyptian bondage, and the hope of an Exodus became a central theme in African-American piety. Central too was an identification with Christ's suffering. The emancipation of the slaves in the whirlwind of war seemed at first the dream of Exodus come true, but the Promised Land did not materialize for blacks in the post-war South. Hope for an Exodus and belief that African Americans had a Christlike mission of redemptive suffering persisted.

Evangelicalism, Fundamentalism, Holiness, and Pentecostalism

In the late nineteenth and early twentieth centuries, both black and white Protestants were touched by yet another wave of radical evangelicalism, which sparked fresh controversies, provoked new divisions, and further diversified the map of American Protestantism. As the Disciples of Christ moved closer to the evangelical mainstream, "Christian" congregations more tenaciously loyal to the movement's early impulses gradually took independent form as the Churches of Christ. Strongest in the South and West, this group grew in the twentieth century into one of the dozen largest Protestant bodies. Millennialism once more produced new groups and tendencies. Both echoes of earlier movements and innovative ideas were to be found in the teachings of the Jehovah's Witnesses, founded by Charles Taze Russell (1852–1916). Critical of such orthodox doctrines as the Trinity and resistant to government authority (e.g., conscription), the Witnesses' most striking feature was the revival of millennialism. Russell taught that the Second Advent had occurred in 1872 and that the final end would come in 1914. More broadly influential were the teachings of John Nelson Darby (1800–1882), the Irish leader of the Plymouth Brethren, who spent much of his later career in the United States promoting dispensationalist premillennialism, a distinctive and innovative scheme for interpreting biblical prophecy. Assuming biblical inerrancy at a time when the inroads of higher criticism were being increasingly felt and undercutting the social optimism of the postmillennialism that had previously prevailed among American evangelicals, it won a considerable audience, especially among Calvinistic Presbyterians and Baptists in the northern states, and provided one of the main distinctive features of the later Fundamentalist movement.[1] More widely influential still, and much more

1. Detailed schemes of how and when the millennium would arrive have differed widely over the centuries, but one can draw a general distinction between "premillennialism" and "postmillennialism." The former typically holds that the millennium is preceded by the rapture of the godly, a terrible time of trials for those left behind, and a literal, miraculous return of Christ. The latter generally sees such cosmic upheavals as occurring only after a millennium in which Christ has reigned spiritually. On this basis, it is often said that premillennialists are pessimists and that postmillennialists are optimists about the future course of ordinary history.

productive of fresh divisions and new denominations, were the varied currents of the holiness movement. With both Reformed and Methodist wings, led at midcentury respectively by Charles Finney and the Methodist laywoman Phoebe Palmer (1807–1874), holiness ideas and practices had a very broad impact, touching the black as well as the white churches. Wesleyan Holiness, with its very clear-cut emphasis on the experience of a "second blessing" and the achievement of a kind of perfection, was more productive of schisms than the Calvinistic branch. The Wesleyan Methodist Church was founded in 1843 by perfectionists whose concept of holiness included antislavery, while the Free Methodist Church was created in 1860 by another band of disillusioned northern Methodists. The major disruptions occurred only toward the end of the century. They drew heavily from Baptists and other groups as well as Methodists, and produced a host of new denominations, themselves prolific of both fresh schisms and mergers. Among the larger of such groups were the Church of God (Anderson, Indiana), organized around 1880 and taking a name intended, as in the earlier Christian movement, to suggest a transcending of humanly created denominations, and the Church of the Nazarene, which had its roots in the 1890s, but took lasting shape only in 1908. Some of the new groups combined a holiness orientation with a special missionary emphasis. The Salvation Army, which arrived in the United States from Britain in 1880, centered its work on urban evangelism and charitable work, while the Christian and Missionary Alliance, created in 1887, combined holiness concerns with an especially strong emphasis on foreign missions. Holiness denominations appeared among blacks as well as whites, the most notable being the Church of God in Christ, organized in the 1890s by the Mississippi Baptists Charles Harrison Mason (1866–1961) and Charles Price Jones (1865–1949).

Especially after the Azusa Street revival in Los Angeles in 1906, many holiness groups were swept into Pentecostalism,[2] among them

2. "Pentecostalism," like Puritanism, Pietism, and Evangelicalism, comes in many forms. A distinctive feature of the movement is its emphasis on

the Church of God in Christ, which in the twentieth century grew to surpass in size all other black churches except the National Baptist Convention, U.S.A. The Azusa Street meetings, presided over by the black preacher William J. Seymour (1870–1922), also exemplified an impulse in the holiness and pentecostal movements, as in radical evangelical movements of an earlier time, to breach the barriers of race. Here too, however, efforts to bridge the racial gap had limited success, as the Pentecostal churches tended themselves to divide along racial lines. At the same time, Pentecostalism was doctrinally fractured by the "finished work" controversy, which generally divided the movement along the older Reformed/Wesleyan divide, and the Oneness movement, which challenged Trinitarian doctrine and baptismal practice. The Assemblies of God, organized in 1914, eventually became the largest of the white Pentecostal denominations. The Church of God (Cleveland, Tennessee), first organized as a Holiness body in the 1880s, also grew in the twentieth century into one of the largest Pentecostal denominations. The Pentecostal Holiness Church, organized initially in 1898, subsequently drew together through a series of mergers several groups whose Pentecostalism was rooted in the Wesleyan tradition. The Pentecostal Assemblies of the World was formed as early as 1906 or 1907 and reorganized in 1918 as the organizational center of Oneness Pentecostalism. After a complicated history of failed attempts to sustain a biracial membership, the church became and remains predominantly black. The largest Oneness denomination, the United Pentecostal Church, was organized only in 1945, through a merger of predominantly white Oneness groups.

"speaking in tongues," i.e., speech that is generally regarded by believers as a divine language they speak only because the Holy Spirit enables them to do so. *Glossolalia* has occurred, however, in a wide range of Christian and other religious movements besides Pentecostalism, and Pentecostals, who do not all interpret the significance of the phenomenon in identical ways, have many doctrinal, liturgical, ethical, and organizational convictions beyond a concern with "speaking in tongues."

Unitarianism, Transcendentalism, Romantic Traditionalism,
and Lutheran Orthodoxy

Complex as were the divisions wrought in American Protestantism
by the currents of radical evangelicalism and the encounter of blacks
and whites, they by no means exhausted the process of diversifica-
tion of American Protestantism during this period. It also moved
along quite different lines, which intersected with evangelical patterns at some points, but sharply diverged from them at others. The
religious rationalism of the Enlightenment, generally in retreat in
early nineteenth-century American Christianity, found an enduring
presence in the very heart of Puritan New England, where Unitarianism captured many of the parishes of the established Congregational
churches and became the prevailing view at Harvard. The organization of the American Unitarian Association in 1825 marked the beginning of independent denominational existence. Led by Boston's
William Ellery Channing (1780–1842), Unitarianism never became a
widely popular movement, yet it attracted much of early nineteenth-
century New England's cultural elite—most notably Ralph Waldo
Emerson (1803–1882)—and thereby indirectly influenced the lives of
millions. Emerson, who began his career as a Unitarian minister, but
became the leading spokesman for the Transcendentalist movement,
also exemplifies the way Romanticism displaced the older rationalism along Unitarianism's cutting edge.

On the one side, such a Romantic sensibility could lead in the
direction of an attraction to religious traditions more venerable and
corporatist than those typical of American evangelicalism. Among
the Transcendentalists, there were converts to Roman Catholicism, most notably Orestes Brownson (1803–1876) and Isaac Hecker
(1819–1888), while within New England Protestantism generally there
developed a complex fascination with Rome, which also yielded
some additional converts. Within the Episcopal Church, especially at
the General Theological Seminary in New York, there developed in
the 1840s a strong sympathy for the Oxford movement in the Church
of England, and throughout the period there was a running battle

within the denomination between High Church and evangelical parties. A combination of Romanticism and traditionalism was also evident in the important theological movement developed in the mid-nineteenth century at the Mercersburg, Pennsylvania, seminary of the German Reformed Church, under the leadership of John Williamson Nevin (1803–1886) and the German Swiss immigrant Philip Schaff (1819–1893). The American Society of Church History, organized under Schaff's leadership in the 1880s, when he was teaching at the Union Theological Seminary in New York, also reflected his broadly affirmative view of the Christian past. Meanwhile, more under the influence of an immigrant-born traditionalism than of Romanticism, Lutherans in the United States moved away from an "American Lutheranism" exemplified by Samuel Simon Schmucker (1799–1873) toward a renewed emphasis on the German language and Lutheran orthodoxy. The Missouri Synod, organized in 1847 and led by Carl F. W. Walther (1811–1887), continues as a bastion of theological conservatism, as does the Christian Reformed Church, established by Dutch immigrants in Michigan in 1857. Another immigrant group, the Evangelical Church Union of the West, which later helped form the Evangelical Synod of North America, embodied on the other hand more irenic tendencies in German Protestantism, combining pietistic strands from both the Lutheran and Reformed traditions. From its ranks in the twentieth century would come two of America's most prominent theologians, the brothers Reinhold (1892–1971) and H. Richard (1894–1962) Niebuhr.

New Age Piety, Theosophy, and Eastern Influences

If Romanticism at times fostered traditionalism, in other cases, as in the instance of Transcendentalism, it led away from historic forms of Christianity toward an eclectic sensibility that displayed, along with much else, an openness to the (then little known in the United States) world of Asian religions. As such, it anticipated an enduring and increasingly important strand of American religion, variously

labeled as harmonial or New Age piety, with its optimistic emphasis
on the possibilities of worldly and spiritual well-being to be won by
inner attunement with a harmonious cosmos. This tendency stands
in a complex relationship with the earlier world of radical evangelicalism, from which it both drew and departed. The Theosophi-
cal Society, organized in 1875 in New York by the Russian immigrant
Helena Petrovna Blavatsky (1831–1891) and led after her death in 1891
by Annie Wood Besant (1847–1933), was distinctive in its considerable borrowing from Buddhism and most especially Hinduism,
yet it echoed as well the beliefs and practices of an earlier American occultism and spiritualism. The Church of Christ (Science),
chartered in 1879, was markedly innovative in its doctrines, organization, and practices. Yet its founder, Mary Baker Eddy (1821–1910),
was closely familiar with antecedent traditions of spiritual healing
in New England Protestantism, and her doctrine of the Father-Mother
God echoed in some ways the dual-gendered godhead of Shakerism.
Harmonial piety, like radical evangelicalism, also produced many seceders and breakaway movements. A revised version of Christian Science was developed and given enduring form by the Unity School of
Christianity, founded by Charles (1854–1948) and Myrtle (1845–1931)
Fillmore in Kansas City in 1889. Another important line of connection runs from the thought of Emanuel Swedenborg, which, quite
apart from its institutionalization in the American branches of the
London-originated Church of the New Jerusalem, widely influenced
both Transcendentalism and more popular spiritualistic and healing movements. The distinctive religious ideas of Henry James, Sr.
(1811–1882), were greatly influenced by Swedenborg and were in turn
highly formative for his son William (1842–1910), whose own religious thought developed the broad harmonial tendency in complex
and creative ways. Meanwhile, public awareness in the United States
of Asian religions was much advanced by the World's Parliament of
Religions, held in Chicago in 1893. A particularly strong impression
was made by the Hindu Swami Vivekananda (1863–1902), whose mo-
nistic teachings were further promoted by the Vedanta Society, organized in 1897. The arrival in San Francisco in 1899 of two perma-

nent missionary priests of the Jodo Shinshu or True Pure Land School of Buddhism marked the formal organization of Buddhist life among immigrants from Japan and created an enduring organization, which in the 1940s renamed itself the Buddhist Churches of America.

Liberal Protestant Theology

The liberal theology that flourished within mainline Protestantism in the latter decades of the nineteenth century and the early decades of the twentieth grew out of the older traditions of Puritan and evangelical orthodoxy, in conversation with developments in European Protestant thought, above all in Germany. Here too, the broad influence of Romanticism also produced impulses toward both a recovery of a corporatist traditionalism and an emphasis on a practically minded harmonialism. Already in Horace Bushnell (1802–1876), an heir to the New England theological tradition, there appeared at midcentury an emphasis on the immanence of God and the poetic character of religious language that laid the groundwork for later developments. Newman Smyth's (1843–1925) contention, early in the twentieth century, that the age of Protestantism had passed and that the future lay in reunion with a Catholicism soon to be transformed by Modernism, expressed—albeit atypically—the impulse toward a renewed emphasis on corporatism and tradition, though only on the basis of an immanentalist assumption about the development of tradition. At the same time, the confidence of Washington Gladden (1836–1918), the most popular prophet of the Social Gospel, that the deepening conflict between labor and capital could be resolved by conciliation and cooperation expressed the harmonial tendency in social form. Such emphases reflected, on the one side, a growing stress on the teachings of Jesus as the norm for Christian social ethics, and on the other the optimistic metaphysics of philosophical idealism. Resistance to such ideas meanwhile added further diversity—and sometimes intense controversy—to the world of

American Protestantism, as conservatives within some denominations sought to oust liberals from the ministry and the seminary faculties or, as in the case of the General Assembly of Presbyterian Church (U.S.A.) in 1910, to commit their churches formally to the defense of the "Five Points" of biblical inerrancy, the Virgin Birth, the satisfactionary theory of the Atonement, the bodily Resurrection, and the miracles of Jesus. At the same time, especially after 1900, challenges were raised within Modernist circles themselves, sometimes under the rising influence of philosophical pragmatism, about the adequacy of the older philosophical idealism.

Protestantism, Anti-Catholicism, and the Quest for a Holy Commonwealth

In the face of all this diversity, the impulse to forge consensus and build a holy commonwealth, so important in early Puritan New England, by no means disappeared entirely. It has been argued that there emerged from the Revolutionary era a broadly shared and independently institutionalized civil religion that gave doctrinal and ritual expression to the idea of American's divine mission even as it avoided the language of religious particularity, but this exaggerates the initial differentiation of such national faith from Christianity, broadly conceived, and at the same time understates the degree to which religious articulations of national purpose were in the nineteenth century politically contested. In the American two-party system, it is broadly true—though of course with many exceptions and complications, above all with respect to race—that one party (successively the Federalists, Whigs, and Republicans) has tended to emphasize collective order, common morality, and privilege while the other (initially the Jeffersonian Republicans, then the Democrats) has stressed diversity, freedom, and equality. The informal Protestant establishment generally tended in this era to work through the former party to effect its religious goals. Opposition to the rising influence of Roman Catholics, who generally affiliated with the Democratic Party, was a major preoccupation of politically organized Protestantism, especially in the northern states where immigration was concentrated. In the late 1840s and early 1850s, as the Whig party was disintegrating over the slavery question, it seemed for a time that the Know Nothings, with their focus on nativism and anti-Catholicism, might emerge as their successor, though in the end it was the Republicans, who focused primarily on restricting the expansion of slavery, who assumed that role. The resulting regional polarization on the slavery issue split Protestants politically, as southern white Protestants became the most loyal of Democrats, even as the older religious polarization persisted in the North, with the Republican Party at times recommending itself as the opponent of "Rum, Romanism, and Rebellion."

Much has sometimes been made of the voluntary association as the instrumentality though which mainline American Protestantism, once deprived of state support, sought, with considerable success, to build consensus and achieve collective goals. Certainly Protestants organized during this period associations for almost every imaginable purpose, and these no doubt played a vital role in fostering lay involvement in Christian work generally. Many of these, however, including numerous domestic missionary societies, the American Bible Society (1816), and the American Tract Society (1823), typically led by Congregationalists and Presbyterians, aimed mostly at spreading modern evangelicalism across the widely expanding nation and typically did not engage divisive social issues. The American Missionary Association was founded in 1846 in large measure because the older American Home Missionary Society (1826) sought to avoid the question of slavery. Such associations also tended to give way, as the century advanced, to more strictly denominational organizations imbedded in increasingly bureaucratic structures. Meanwhile, movements devoted to religiously based social reform tended, as they developed, to abandon a purely persuasive strategy in favor of attempts to build political support for using the coercive power of the state. The American Anti-Slavery Society (1833), under the leadership of William Lloyd Garrison (1805–1879), was militant but antipolitical, whereas the American and Foreign Anti-Slavery Society (1840) endorsed political means and in the ensuing two decades helped force the issue into the political system, where it eventually produced a decisive showdown in 1860. The temperance movement similarly moved, broadly speaking, from limited efforts to persuade individuals to later attempts to mobilize political support for state action. The Anti-Saloon League (1893), based particularly in the Methodist churches of both North and South, was a single-issue pressure group that proved highly effective at moving the country to the adoption in 1919 of the Eighteenth Amendment to the constitution, outlawing the production and consumption of alcoholic beverages. Even the more inclusive and politically oriented of these voluntary associations seldom recruited many Roman Catholics, and the agenda they promoted was typically seen as a specifically Protestant effort struggling against Catholic indifference or resistance.

American Protestantism also achieved a certain coherence and sense of common purpose during this period through an increasingly self-conscious emphasis on the central place of women in Christianity—and here too an opposition to Roman Catholicism was often a central element. No doubt, the question of women's participation in church life and in the wider society was in one sense an additional source of Protestant division. Controversy swirled over women's public praying at revivalistic meetings, their expanding role as itinerant preachers, and their rising demands for access to the ordained ministry. The dividing line between moderate and more radical evangelicals often paralleled the line between those who welcomed a wider role for women and those who opposed it. The women's rights movement, launched at the Woman's Rights Convention, held at Seneca Falls, New York, in 1848 under the leadership of Elizabeth Cady Stanton (1815–1902), was often as controversial as the radical abolitionist movement of William Lloyd Garrison from which it had emerged. When Stanton, who began as a moderate evangelical but eventually became persuaded, like Garrison, of the reactionary force of traditional religion, published in the 1890s a strong critique of the Bible's treatment of women, she was largely repudiated even by fellow feminists. Nevertheless, there was among American Protestants a widely shared belief that the elevation of women was a critical measure of religious progress and a central virtue of American Protestantism. Initially, a prevailing emphasis on the ethos of domesticity, which sharply separated the spheres of men and women, confined women's work to home and church, at least for moderate evangelicals. As the century advanced, however, this was decreasingly true. In the career of Frances Willard (1839–1898), leader of the Women's Christian Temperance Union, organized in 1874, the idea of taking the home into the world and thereby taming male vice with female virtue allowed for a greater militancy. Within the black churches, Methodism meanwhile produced a series of influential woman preachers, while among the Baptists, Nannie Burroughs (1879–1961) made the Woman's Convention, an auxiliary of the National Baptist Convention, a major force in black church life. Meanwhile, even Protestants who disagreed on the precise role appropriate for women in church and society could agree that Catholicism was an impediment to Christianity's ongoing elevation of women. The celibate priesthood and the salient role of nuns figured in anti-Catholicism as a reactionary assault both on domesticity and on appropriate public activity for women.

Roman Catholicism and American Society

Faced, on the one hand, by the prevailing Protestant tendency to define public morality in anti-Catholic terms, and on the other by sharp papal rejection of the kind of non-Catholic liberal-capitalist nation-state that the United States exemplified, American Catholics were not well-situated to advance their own view of public order. Most basically, American Catholics responded to their circum-

stances, which included the absorption of wave after wave of typically poor, working-class immigrants, by building a separate institutional world that included not only churches, but also schools,
hospitals, and charitable associations. Relatively rapid naturalization
and easy access—for white males—to the franchise meant, however,
that Catholics quickly established a political presence, primarily
through the Democratic Party, and were thus able to defend their in-
terests, particularly at the local level. At the same time, American
Catholicism tended at times to take on the color of its Protestant
environment, as in early nineteenth-century "trusteeism," in which
lay Catholics in some places resisted episcopal authority and sought
to run their parishes on essentially congregationalist terms. A few
Catholics, moreover, flying in the face of the prevailing opinion
among both American Protestants and European Catholics that
Catholicism and the United States were ill-suited to one another, argued that Roman Catholicism in fact provided the only sound foun-
dation for American institutions and that American institutions
provided an ideal environment for Catholic flourishing. Initially,
these ideas were advanced primarily by native-born converts from
Protestantism, most especially Orestes Brownson, who contended
that the American civil order rested on natural law foundations that
a subjectivist Protestantism had abandoned but Catholicism maintained, and Isaac Hecker, the founder of the Paulists, who believed
the separation of church and state facilitated the working of the Holy
Spirit among the faithful. Embraced in the late nineteenth century
by such leaders as John Joseph Keane (1839–1918), John Ireland
(1838–1918), and, to a lesser extent, by Cardinal Gibbons (1834–1921),
as part of a broader effort to reduce the isolation of Catholicism in
American public life, such ideas aroused the suspicions of the Vatican and in 1899, in *Testem Benevolentiae*, Leo XIII (1810–1903;
pope, 1878–1903) condemned "Americanism," somewhat indefinitely,
but nonetheless effectively. By 1907, when Pius X (1835–1914; pope,
1903–1914) in *Pascendi Gregis* condemned Modernism, the more liberal wing of American Catholicism was clearly in retreat.

A Growing American Role in Foreign Missions
and International Politics

Meanwhile, as the century advanced, American Protestants turned
their attention and energies increasingly to the cause of foreign missions. Already in the early nineteenth century, the American Board
of Commissioners of Foreign Missions (ABCFM), organized in 1810
under New England Congregationalist leadership but for a time
mobilizing as well the missionary efforts of the Dutch Reformed,
German Reformed, and New School Presbyterian Churches, was
(next to the American Bible Society) the best-funded of the American Protestant voluntary associations of the antebellum period. Even
so it was a small anticipation of what mainline American Protestant
missions became at their peak, in the half-century after 1880. With
some ninety missionary societies at work, Americans by 1900 de-
ployed twice as many missionaries as Continental Europeans and by
1910 had surpassed the British as well. Here too, of course, there were
debates and divisions, as American mission theorists quarreled over
the relation of "Christianization and civilization," as the movement became more and more organized along denominational lines,
and, toward the close of the period, as such groups as premillennialists working through the Moody Bible Institute and other training
schools more and more challenged the work of the mainline Protestant churches touched by Modernism. At the same time, the missionary movement was also a powerful vehicle for the expression
of common purpose and reflection on American national destiny.
Women, crucial from the outset as domestic supporters of the missionary enterprise, became over the nineteenth century increasingly
prominent workers in the field, and the belief that Protestantism ele-
vated the place of women significantly shaped the missionary movement abroad, as it did domestic reform. The Congregationalists who
launched the ABCFM drew on the millennial hopes nourished in
New England by Edwards and evident both in the Revolutionary
movement and in the early missionary efforts of Samuel Hopkins,

believing that through their efforts America might have a special place in a new work of the Spirit. A prevailing optimism was also evident at century's end in the slogan of the Student Volunteer Movement for Foreign Missions, organized in 1888 and led by John R. Mott (1865–1955) and Robert Speer (1867–1947), which called for "the evangelization of the world in this generation."

These hopes and efforts were at once enabled and complicated by their entanglement in the rising global power of the American nation-state and its deep complicity in worldwide patterns of racial domination. Toward the end of this period, the United States had not only secured its modern continental borders, but had established a growing political, military, economic, cultural, and religious presence well beyond the North American continent. The war with Spain (1898) not only entrenched American power in a new way in the Caribbean, where the United States took control of Puerto Rico, but also, through the American occupation of the Philippines, made the United States an Asian power. Indeed, the central role of the United States in the emerging global order was apparent in the building of the Panama Canal, completed in 1914, which brought the Atlantic and Pacific worlds into closer touch with one another. The entry of the United States into the First World War and its central involvement in shaping the consequent peace were a further extension of this process.

The Race Issue

American missions grew and flourished as American world power grew and flourished. At the same time, they were, as they had been from the outset, deeply tied, however unwillingly at times, to patterns of racial hierarchy central to the international order. Already in the early nineteenth century, American missionary interest in Africa had been compromised by its close ties to efforts to rid the United States of its free black population. Samuel J. Mills, Jr. (1783–1818), one of the key early leaders of the American missionary effort, died in 1818 returning from West Africa, where he had gone under the auspices of the recently founded American Colonization Society (ACS), to advance a plan to establish a missionary colony of American blacks. The work of the ACS drew upon the same missionary impulse that moved Samuel Hopkins and enjoyed the support of some African Americans, most notably the African-Amerindian shipowner Paul Cuffe (1759–1817), who hoped both to advance Christianity in Africa and provide a home for freed slaves. Though intended by some of its founders to advance the cause of antislavery, the ACS also drew crucial support from southern slaveholders and political leaders eager to eliminate the threat to slave society that a growing population of free blacks was thought to represent, and it ultimately rested on the premise that the United States was and must remain "a white man's country." The ACS drew sustained support from mainline Protestantism in the antebellum period, despite its vigorous rejection by most black church leaders and its ringing denunciation by the abolitionist movement, and even Abraham Lincoln long held that ex-slaves must be colonized outside the United States. The failure, during the post–Civil War period of Reconstruction, to build in the ex-slave states a new biracial order, led by the end of the century to the establishment of a strict system of racial segregation and hierarchy, which took shape even as the European powers were consolidating their hold on Africa and advancing their domination of Asia. Mainline Protestantism's difficulty in extracting the concept of American destiny from its embeddedness in ideas of racial hierarchy rendered ambiguous its growing role in the globalization of Christianity. Some African-American Christian leaders, most notably AME bishop and prominent black nationalist Henry McNeal Turner (1834–1915), denounced the United States as irredeemably racist, urged African Americans to identify with Africa, and, sounding once again the Exodus theme, urged blacks with resources to emigrate there. Others, forging a distinctive millennial tradition of their own, hoped for a divine reversal of the prevailing global racial order. When Josiah Strong (1847–1916), in Darwinian tones, spoke in the 1880s of the destiny of Anglo-Saxons (understood as bearers of the traditions of Protestantism and social and political liberalism) to dominate the future, the black theologian Theophilus Gould Steward (1843–1924) replied that biblical prophecy showed the age of the Europeans was soon to end and that in its place would arise a world order dominated by Christians of color.

The First World War

The participation of the United States in the First World War brought into sharp relief the complexities of America's developing global role. Such Christians as William Jennings Bryan (1860–1925), three-time Democratic Party nominee for the presidency and evangelical social liberal, who believed that America's role in the world was to serve as a moral example, rejected the call to war even as they had earlier resisted the imperialist impulse. Others, such as eminent Social Gospel leader Walter Rauchenbusch (1861–1918), who had endorsed the war with Spain, could not embrace the war against Germany. Once war was declared, most American Christians energetically supported the effort, though some tried at the same time to resist the ensuing surge of national chauvinism the war unleashed. African Americans were aware that Woodrow Wilson (1856–1924; president, 1913–1921), the earnest Presbyterian who led America into a fight to "make the world safe for democracy," was also a southern-born segregationist who insisted the etiquette of strict racial hierarchy be observed by the federal government in Washington, D.C. Wilson's fellow Presbyterian, the prominent black pastor Francis Grimké (1850–1937), who supported the war and rejoiced in the Allied victory, nonetheless thought the Allies had fought in part to keep the world safe for white supremacy—as evidenced he thought by their cool attitude toward Japan, which seemed to him, as to many other African Americans, a champion of the darker races generally. Grimké, like Steward, hoped for and believed in the imminent appearance of a new global Christianity purged of racial injustice.

CHAPTER 3

A Global Power

Notwithstanding the failure of the United States to enter the League of Nations, American participation in the First World War and in the Versailles Conference marked a new level of international engagement, which has grown exponentially in succeeding decades. American Christianity has been deeply influenced by the nation's growing immersion in global geopolitics. Conceptions of American mission and destiny have more and more turned on the United States' place in the international economic, social, and political order, and the overseas use of American military power has alternately united and deeply divided American Christians. At the same time, the decline after 1930 in the overseas missionary efforts of the older denominations of the Protestant establishment has been more than counterbalanced by the growing international efforts of a wide range of other American Christian groups, most especially conservative evangelicals and Pentecostals, and such American-born bodies as the Mormons, the Seventh-Day Adventists, and the Jehovah's Witnesses. As Americans have more and more gone out into the world, the world has also increasingly come to the United States. After a forty-year lull between 1924 and 1965, a massive new wave of immigration has once again redrawn the map of American Christianity and widened the scope of religious diversity. The challenge of religious pluralism is no longer centered primarily on peoples of European origin and overwhelmingly Christian (or, otherwise, Jewish) loyalties, but on a global mix of races and religions with increasingly salient non-European and non-Christian components. Within the Christian population, Latinos/as constitute the largest stream of immigrants and are placing their mark on the worlds of both Catholicism and Protestantism in the United States. Their presence, as part of a wider Latin American and Caribbean immigration involving more than Spanish-speakers and including many persons of African descent, marks a reconnection of American Christianity to the wider Atlantic world in which it first emerged. At the same time, Muslim immigration to the United States and deepening American engagement with the Islamic world globally have tied American Christianity ever more closely to the centuries-old history of Christian-Muslim conflict, collaboration, and confluence in the Mediterranean world. Both this Latino/a and wider Atlantic immigration and this renewed engagement with Islam have significantly affected the enduring gap between blacks and whites in the United States, which, like the definition of religious pluralism and the articulation of shared goals and values, has remained in this period a central problematic for American Christianity.

From Protestant Hegemony to "Protestant-Catholic-Jew"

The period in the immediate aftermath of World War I was marked by intense social strife outside the churches, including major strikes and race riots, and intense controversy among and within the churches. Earlier divisions within the Protestant mainstream had deepened during the war and now erupted into fierce conflict, especially among Presbyterians and Baptists. The World's Christian Fundamentals Association, organized toward the war's close, mobilized a wide constituency of antimodernist evangelicals to resist the inroads of Modernism within the churches and evolution in the schools. The movement, which saw itself as fighting to defend the bedrock convictions on which Christian America rested, received a name in 1920 when Curtis Lee Laws (1868–1946) coined the term "fundamentalism." A beleaguered Protestant counterthrust to forces of change was also evident in the reemergence of the Ku Klux Klan. Originally formed in the post–Civil War South as a white terrorist organization fighting to overturn the biracial governments of the Reconstruction era, the Klan reappeared in 1915 and, broadening its agenda to include anti-Catholicism and anti-Semitism alongside its previous animus against blacks, now won a strong following in the Middle West as well as the South. Klan activists within the Democratic Party were in part responsible for a bitterly divisive struggle that blocked the nomination of Governor Alfred Smith (1873–1944) of New York, a Roman Catholic, as the party's presidential candidate in 1924. Marcus Garvey (1887–1940), the Jamaican black nationalist who had moved the headquarters of his Universal Negro Improvement Association to New York in 1916, in some ways seemed to concede America to the Klan and its allies. Sounding many of the same themes as Henry McNeal Turner and enjoying considerable support from black Christians, he too called on African Americans to identify themselves with Africa rather than the United States and to do what they could to resist colonialism and promote the creation of a powerful black empire. Yet Garveyism, which quickly became the largest mass movement in African-American history, clearly constituted a powerful challenge to the hegemony of the older white Protestantism. Meanwhile, Horace Kallen (1882–1974), an immigrant rabbi's son, Harvard-educated pragmatist, and secular Zionist, argued forcefully and influentially that, in the either/or cultural wars of the moment, authentic American tradition was not represented by "Kultur Klux Klan" but by "cultural pluralism." Such "hyphenated Americans" as Jews in the United States, who were determined to be at once both Americans and Jews, were not for Kallen aberrant, but rather normative citizens and the true bearers of the American tradition.

In the face of such challenges, the forces of mainstream Protestantism, particularly when they were able to work with some degree of unity, were still able decisively to shape public policy according to their own convictions. This is clear in the triumph of prohibition and more indirectly evident in the ratification of the Nineteenth Amendment, granting the franchise to women in 1920. It also appears, perhaps most importantly, in the Immigration Quota Act of 1924, which restricted the annual number of newcomers to 2 percent of the members of each nationality already present in the United States at the time of the 1890 census—a date before the northern European Protestant majority had been eroded by the flood of immigration from southern and eastern Europe. When Alfred Smith finally achieved the Democratic presidential nomination in 1928, moreover, he was decisively beaten in the election. Meanwhile Marcus Garvey, convicted of mail fraud in relation to his back-to-Africa Black Star steamship line, was jailed in 1925 and deported two years later.

Still, there were limits on the ability of Protestants in general and certainly conservative evangelicals in particular to shape American life as fully as they once had. At the Scopes trial in 1925, where a Tennessee schoolteacher was convicted of breaking the state's laws against teaching evolution, Fundamentalists won the legal battle but lost the more important cultural contest when William Jennings Bryan, now the standard bearer of the struggle to defend the Bible, was widely seen to have been humiliated by the skeptical lawyer Clarence Darrow (1857–1938). In the United States after 1925, Protestant Christianity could no longer see itself as exclusively as it once had as the nation's religion, and intra-Protestant diversity could no longer serve as the main standard of acceptable diversity. What emerged, however, was not quite the cultural pluralism of Horace Kallen, but something closer to the pattern most memorably sketched by another Jewish social critic, Will Herberg (1906–1977), who argued in the 1950s that Protestantism, Catholicism, and Judaism had all come to stand as acceptable forms of faith in America, thereby creating a "triple melting pot" in which immigrant diversity was reduced to a simple religious difference. No doubt, the status of the three faiths was less equal and more contested than Herberg supposed, and the submergence of ethnicity in religion less complete than he imagined. Nevertheless, after the mid-1920s the older Protestant mainstream did have to acknowledge in a new way the established presence in American life of Catholicism and Judaism and, until events of the 1960s overturned this formulation, the phrase "Protestant-Catholic-Jew" was the working definition of American religious diversity. All of this was deeply conditioned by the curtailment of immigration during this period and the resulting relative stability of ethnic and religious balance within the American population.

Convergence and Consensus among the Protestant Churches

Within the world of Protestantism itself, stability and consensus also seemed more prevalent than in the preceding period, and here too the decline in immigration fostered processes of convergence and assimilation. The bitter Fundamentalist-Modernist battles receded after 1925, and the emergence in the 1930s of an American version of Neo-Orthodoxy, which remained however closer in its basic methods to the older Modernism than did its European counterpart, gave the somewhat misleading appearance that the previous division had been more or less permanently overcome. The Niebuhr brothers, who played an important role in moving the Evangelical Synod away from a reliance on the German language toward a broader engagement with American public life, exemplified the movement of immigrant Protestantism into the mainstream. Reinhold Niebuhr at Union Theological Seminary and H. Richard Niebuhr at Yale taught at two of the historic centers of Anglo-Protestant thought in America, and while Richard was more deeply influential within academic theology, Reinhold in the 1940s and 1950s became one of the leading public intellectuals in the United States. In part under the influence of Marxism, Reinhold Niebuhr moved away from the harmonialism of the older Social Gospel toward a view of class conflict as a struggle for justice in which violence is sometimes required. As the focus of his attention shifted away from the industrial order toward the rise of fascism, the Second World War, and then the Cold War, his "Christian realism" lost some, though by no means all, of its earlier radicalism and became increasingly a defense of America's widening global role in the defense of pluralistic democracy.

Consensus rather than division also seemed the prevailing force in the world of mainstream Protestant institutions, as there began a series of mergers that throughout the twentieth century reversed many of the schisms of the nineteenth century. At times, such mergers not only gathered together churches of broadly common origins, but sometimes reached across ethnic lines in doing so. In 1934, the Evangelical Synod joined with the German Reformed Church, creating the Evangelical and Reformed Church. Already in 1931, the Congregational Churches, descendants of the Puritans, had joined with smaller groups rooted in the "Christian" movement of the early nineteenth century to form the Christian Congregational Church. These two largely Reformed bodies, one German and one English in origin, joined together in 1957 to create the United Church of Christ. Methodists, in reuniting along regional lines in 1939, also drew in the Methodist Protestants. In forming the United Methodist Church in 1968, they added as well the Evangelical United Brethren, itself a merger of two smaller groups of German origin. The most distinctively Scottish of the larger Presbyterian denominations in the United States, the United Presbyterian Church, formed in 1858, had long been the primary bearer in America of the traditions of the Covenanters and the Seceders. In 1958, it merged with the major branch of northern Presbyterianism, the Presbyterian Church, U.S.A., to form the United Presbyterian Church, U.S.A. In the mid-1980s, this denomination in turn merged with the Presbyterian Church in the United States, the major southern branch of the tradition, to form the Presbyterian Church (U.S.A.). Lutherans also overcame a history of ethnic as well as regional differences in the century-long series of unions that eventually produced the Evangelical Lutheran Church in America (ELCA) in 1988. A merger of three independent Lutheran bodies in 1918 had created the United Lutheran Synod. Strongest in the eastern states and somewhat more liberal than other Lutheran bodies, it was the first Lutheran denomination that could be counted a part of the informal Protestant establishment. In 1962, it had merged with the Augustana Lutheran Church, which was Swedish in origin, as well as with two other bodies of Danish and Finnish origins, to form the Lutheran Church in America (LCA). Meanwhile, just two years before, the American Lutheran Church (ALC) had combined in one denomination a number of other Lutheran bodies, German, Norwegian, and Danish in origin, primarily based in the midwestern states. The LCA and ALC joined to create the ELCA, drawing in as well a small seceding fragment of the Missouri Synod, which had maintained its independence and strict loyalty to its conservative Lutheran origins. On a much smaller scale, two liberal bodies formed as anti-Calvinist movements in the early national period joined in 1961 to form the Unitarian Universalist Association.

Throughout this entire period, there have also been within mainline Protestantism tendencies toward even more inclusive bodies than these. In part, building on nineteenth-century patterns of interdenominational voluntary associations, particularly the Evangelical Alliance, this wider Protestant ecumenism has taken the form of church federations fostering collaboration among independent bodies. The Federal Council of Churches of Christ in America, founded in 1908, drew together over thirty Protestant churches around an agenda that placed considerable emphasis on Social Gospel concerns. Merged with other groups and reorganized in 1950 as the National Council of the Churches of Christ in the United States of America, this cooperative body reached well beyond the Protestant mainstream, already by the early 1960s embracing a range of Eastern Orthodox churches whose agenda was at times significantly different from that of mainstream Protestantism. A desire within conservative Protestant circles to create a counterweight to these more liberal bodies produced in 1941 the American Council of Churches, a small and narrowly Fundamentalist body, and more significantly, in 1942, the larger and more inclusive National Association of Evangelicals. Some Protestants meanwhile aspired to go beyond church federations to form a single Protestant church embracing at the very least the core denominations of the old Protestant establishment. When in 1960 Presbyterian leader Eugene Carson Blake (1906–1985) and Episcopal

Bishop James Pike (1913–1969) called Episcopalians, Presbyterians, Methodists, and the United Church of Christ to join in conversations toward a "Reformed and Catholic Church in the U.S.A.," it seemed such hopes might materialize. The ensuing Consultation on Church Union, later renamed the Church of Christ Uniting, has not created such a result and is unlikely to do so in the near future. It has, however, promoted a widening practice of intercommunion and the mutual recognition of ministries among a growing number of mainstream Protestant denominations.

Catholicism's New Place

The early 1960s, when the Blake-Pike proposal most excited Protestant ecumenists, also saw the convening of the Second Vatican Council and the opening of new ecumenical conversations even across the old Catholic-Protestant line. By this time, American Catholicism was winning more warmly from many Protestants the acknowledgment of its new place in American life that had been given rather grudgingly since the mid-1920s. The closing of immigration gradually freed American Catholic energies from the demanding task of institutionally absorbing wave after wave of typically poor newcomers. At the same time, Catholics increasingly worked their way into the middle class—and beyond—and, with the vast expansion of American higher education after World War II, began in larger number to attend non-Catholic colleges and universities. No doubt, Catholicism in America still remained for the most part confined to its own institutional world and recurrently subject to attack by outsiders as an alien body in a democratic society. A flourishing Neo-Thomism served as a vehicle for older Americanist claims that, in the face of Protestant and secular subjectivism and relativism, only Catholicism could provide a secure intellectual basis for American public institutions and pursuit of the common good, even as Protestant and other thinkers working in the pragmatist tradition at times attacked Catholics as antidemocratic, medieval-minded authoritarians.

Catholics lamented the failure of the United States to support Mexican Catholicism in the face of a deeply anticlerical regime in the 1920s, then took severe criticism from liberals and the left in the 1930s for their own support of the Franco regime in Spain. Catholic opposition to the growing practice of birth control kept alive some of the gender-focused controversies of previous eras, but the relative quiescence of Protestant and other feminist movements during this period made these issues far less powerful than they had been previously. At the same time, the widespread Depression-era critique of liberal capitalism coincided in part with parallel themes in Catholic social thought reaching as far back as *Rerum Novarum*, the famous encyclical of Pope Leo XIII in 1891, and renewed by Pius XI (1857–1939; pope, 1922–1939) in *Quadragesimo Anno* in 1931. The eclectic and evolving New Deal of President Franklin Roosevelt (1882–1945; president, 1933–1945) also at various points advanced corporatist concepts and social welfare policies espoused since the end of World War I by John A. Ryan (1869–1945) and the National Catholic Welfare Conference. Catholics also provided two-thirds of the membership of the trade unions that secured a new place in American life in the New Deal era, while their strong links to the now-dominant Democratic Party gave Catholics a larger share of influence and important appointments than in any previous administration. Meanwhile, with Dorothy Day (1897–1980) and the Catholic Worker Movement, American Catholicism produced a vigorous nonviolent radical movement unprecedented in Catholic history in the United States, and, even as it recruited increasing numbers of blacks, Catholicism became more active in the struggle against racial discrimination. The careers of Charles E. Coughlin (1891–1979), a radio priest whose promotion of the social encyclicals passed over into a populist anti-Semitism, and Senator Joseph McCarthy (1908–1957), the most controversial and politically aggressive anti-Communist of the 1950s, evidenced in a quite different way Catholicism's increasingly wide-ranging influence in American public life. Finally, the election in 1960 of a Roman Catholic, John F. Kennedy (1917–1963; president, 1961–1963), to the presidency of the United States, his sub-

sequent great popularity, and his tragic death, broke though a powerful symbolic barrier and established in a new way the full legitimacy
of the Catholic presence in America. Of critical importance was the
coincidence of Kennedy's presidency and the convening of the Second Vatican Council. The Council's Declaration on Religious Freedom (1965), drafted by the American Jesuit John Courtney Murray
(1904–1967) and actively promoted by the most prominent American cardinals, fulfilled the Americanists' dream and ended the long-
standing awkwardness of the Roman Catholic Church's acceptance
of the separation of church and state in the United States as a practi-
cal reality but not as a normative practice.

Convergence and Consensus with Judaism

American Judaism in these decades also went through a period of
both internal consolidation and an outward advance in securing its
place in American life. A sharp antagonism had previously existed
between Reform and Orthodox Judaism. This was rooted in a broader
opposition between the older German, more liberal and assimila-
tionist, and more middle-class immigration of the earlier nineteenth
century, and the eastern European, more radical and Zionist, and
more working-class immigration of the late nineteenth and early
twentieth centuries. During these years this opposition was soft-
ened both by the upward social mobility of the Jewish population as
a whole and by the growing strength of the Conservative movement,
which, like the romantic traditionalism of the nineteenth century or
contemporary Protestant Neo-Orthodoxy, sought at once to be traditional and progressive. The Holocaust and the creation of the state
of Israel won even the most reluctant wing of Reform to a Zionist
position, which now became a central point of reference for deepening solidarity among American Jews generally. The rise of anti-
Semitism in the 1930s, promoted by sources as diverse as Henry Ford
(1863–1947) and Father Coughlin, indicated ongoing resistance to the
acceptance of Jews as full partners in the American experiment, but

closer ties with the Protestant establishment, in part through the "goodwill movement," marked a tendency toward the inclusion of Judaism as an accepted element in America's pluralistic religious life. Having largely shifted their votes from an older allegiance to the Republicans to a disproportionate vote for the Democrats, Jews were also part of the governing New Deal coalition. The active support of the Truman administration for the creation of the state of Israel further consolidated this loyalty.

The Consolidation of Orthodox Christianity

Eastern Orthodox Christians were not included in the "Protestant-Catholic-Jew" formula of American religious pluralism and remained almost invisible in American public life during this period. For them too, however, this was a period of consolidation. Though it had earlier antecedents, most importantly in Russian Orthodox missions in Alaska (launched in the late eighteenth century) and the subsequent creation of a West Coast diocese centered in San Francisco, the presence of Eastern Orthodoxy in the United States was primarily rooted in the same eastern European immigration that had transformed Judaism, most especially in the wave of immigrants arriving between 1900 and 1914. Initially, the Russian church exercised a general jurisdiction over all Orthodox Christians in the United States, but the Revolution of 1917 divided Russian Orthodoxy in America into competing wings and, like other immigrant groups, the Orthodox established in America branches of the national churches of the homelands from which they came. Among these, which included the Albanian, Bulgarian, Greek, Romanian, Serbian, and Ukrainian churches, there were in some cases further divisions over political controversies at home or complex jurisdictional relations to other bodies. The total result, especially before 1930, was one of great instability. As the largest of the Orthodox constituencies, the Greeks became one important point of consolidation. The Greek Archdiocese of North and South America, created in

1930, remains the largest of the Orthodox bodies. The second largest, the Orthodox Church of America was recognized as an autocephalous body only in 1970, but its resistance to the authority of Moscow had long made it the most autonomous of the main Orthodox bodies in the United States. St. Vladimir's Seminary in New York, and such thinkers as George Florovsky (1893–1979), John Meyendorf (1926–1992), and Alexander Schmemann (1921–1983), had by the 1960s established an Orthodox intellectual presence in American Christianity. Meanwhile the Orthodox churches also received a considerable accession of Uniate Catholics who, often denied by American prelates the distinctive rites and, most especially, married clergy authorized by Rome in their homelands, had left Roman Catholicism. Further evidence of consolidation among the Orthodox in America is evident in the organization in 1960 of a broad consultative body, the Standing Conference of Canonical Orthodox Bishops in the United States. By 1961, Greek, Romanian, Russian, Serbian, Syrian, and Ukrainian Orthodox Churches, plus the Armenian Church and Polish National Catholic Church, were active and pressing their views in the National Council of Churches.

Christian Minorities of Non-European Origins

The tripartite formulation of Protestant-Catholic-Jew as the normative pluralism in American religion was in practice a recognition, albeit an incomplete one, of the religious diversity present among European Americans only. Part of the newly emerging Orthodox constituency in America, such as the Antiochian Church (Syrian-Lebanese) was, however, not of European origin, nor were Eastern Rite (Uniate) Catholics from the Middle East, most notably Maronites (Lebanese) and Melkites (Syrian). Indeed, it is to be noted that the earliest wave of Middle Eastern immigration to the United States in the late nineteenth and early twentieth centuries was primarily Christian, not Muslim. Also arriving at the same time were members of Eastern Christian churches not in communion with the patriarch at Istanbul. Among these the Armenian Church, which established a diocese in the United States as early as 1898, became during this period the largest Monophysite constituency in America. There has also been in the United States since just before World War I a very small body of adherents of the Assyrian Church of the East (Nestorian Church) and its exiled head moved his headquarters to the United States during World War II. Christians were also to be found during these years among East Asian immigrants to the United States. The Japanese who came to America from the 1880s to 1925 included a significant number of Christians, and additional Japanese immigrants converted in the United States. Japanese-American Christians were placed in internment camps alongside other Japanese Americans during World War II. Immigrants from the Caribbean, though far fewer in number among early twentieth-century immigrants than they would be after 1965, contributed in highly varied ways to the map of African-American Christianity. A Bahamian immigrant, Berlin Martin Nottage (1889–1966), was largely responsible for the development of a small African-American constituency among the Plymouth Brethren, while George Alexander McGuire (1866–1934), an Antiguan and one-time Moravian pastor, then an Episcopal priest, organized the African Orthodox Church in the 1920s, securing episcopal orders from the West Syrian Church of Antioch. Puerto Ricans and Cubans, centered on the East Coast, mostly though not entirely Roman Catholic, joined with a much larger population of Mexican Americans in the Southwest to constitute a sizable Spanish-speaking constituency, yet one with relatively little visibility during this period. All this would change after 1965, when renewed immigration shifted American Christianity, as American religion generally, away from its predominantly European roots.

African-American Religion and the Global Struggle for Racial Justice

Decisive in shaping the context for the post-1965 emergence of a less European America was the changing place of African Americans in the United States. As in previous periods, the (social and religious) distance between blacks and whites remained from the mid-1920s to the mid-1960s a persistent reality in American religious life, pressing beyond the boundaries of diversity and challenging notions of collective purpose—and international role. There were at work in this period, however, powerful currents moving the United States away from the severe system of racial segregation institutionalized in the southern states at the close of the nineteenth century. The restriction of immigration altered the labor market to the advantage of blacks, drawing them to the industrial North and West even as the mechanization of southern agriculture reduced their opportunities in the rural South. The northward and westward migration of the African-American population, heretofore clustered largely in the former slave states of the South, first around the time of World War I and then in much larger numbers during World War II, reduced regional distinctiveness in all respects, including religious. Being able to vote, as they generally could not in the South, blacks had more access to political influence. They also shifted their political affiliations, first in the 1930s and then further in the 1960s, to the Democratic Party. All of this importantly contributed to the passage in the mid-1960s, with conspicuous support from prominent religious leaders, of national legislation which largely eliminated the legal (though scarcely the social, economic, and political) barriers to racial equality in the United States. This movement toward racial inclusion, which seemed to mark a new level of national unity, signaled, however, the end of a time of consensus and consolidation and the beginning of a period in which increased diversity again became the central fact of American religious life.

The African-American Protestant establishment was in many respects more effective during these years in maintaining its preeminence within black America than its white counterpart was in holding its place in the nation's religious life more generally. In the creation in 1933 of the National Fraternal Council of Negro Churches, African-American Protestant leaders created a new vehicle for their own collective efforts. No doubt, the internal migration of blacks upset many older patterns. The various black Methodist denominations (who pursued without success conversations about their possible merger) fared less well than the Baptists, who now became the undisputed central force in African-American religious life. Adam Clayton Powell, Jr. (1908–1972), pastor of the Abyssinian Baptist Church in Harlem and for many years one of only two African-American members of the United States House of Representatives, provides one example of black Baptist influence in American public life. Another is Martin Luther King, Jr. (1929–1968), who served as pastor of the Dexter Avenue Baptist Church in Montgomery, Alabama, and co-pastor of the Ebenezer Baptist Church in Atlanta during the years he headed the Southern Christian Leadership Conference and became the internationally recognized leader of the civil rights movement. As the long career of Thomas A. Dorsey (1899–1993), one-time jazz pianist turned gospel song composer, at Pilgrim Baptist Church in Chicago makes clear, Baptists were also centrally involved in the creative growth of black religious music, though here the deepest energies emerged from Holiness and Pentecostal churches, which became increasingly important as the century advanced. The older churches of the black Protestant establishment were also challenged, on the one side, by new religious movements, such as the Peace Mission Movement of Father Divine (George Baker, 1879–1965), a harmonial teacher believed by his followers to be God incarnate, and the United House of Prayer for All People, an idiosyncratic variation on Pentecostalism founded by the Cape Verdean immigrant Charles Emmanuel "Daddy" Grace (1882–1960). On the other side, they faced growing black interest in Catholicism and, to a much lesser extent, Orthodoxy. The founding in 1920, under the auspices of the Society of the Divine Word, of a seminary (soon located at Bay Saint Louis, Mississippi) for the training of black priests marked a new phase in the long-delayed process of creating an African-American Catholic priesthood, while the migration of blacks to the urban North and West and their political realignment reduced their physical and social distance from the centers of Catholic strength. Out of the Garvey movement, there emerged the African Orthodox Church, while the Jamaican-based Rastafarian movement regarded the Emperor Haile Selassie (1892–1975) of Ethiopia as divine. Traditions other than Christianity also began to exert increasing attraction for some African Americans. The Church of God and Saints of Christ, founded in 1896 by William Saunders Crowdy (1847–1908), believed blacks to be descended from the lost tribes of Israel and blended Jewish practices with Holiness teachings. The Commandment Keepers Congregation of the Living God, organized by Wentworth A. Matthew (1892–1973) in the 1920s, saw African Americans as Ethiopian Hebrews who needed to recover their ancient adherence to Judaism. The Moorish Science Temple, founded around 1913 by a southern black who took the name Noble Drew Ali (Timothy Drew, 1886–1929), taught that African Americans were truly Moroccans, but the movement's idiosyncratic Holy Koran was an eclectic blend of harmonial piety, Masonic symbols, Eastern religions, and Islam. The Nation of Islam, founded in the 1930s and given its enduring form by Elijah Muhammad (1897–1975), also combined a claim that Islam was the true religion of blacks with an idiosyncratic theology emphasizing the demonic origins of whites and a coming racial apocalypse. Meanwhile Muslim immigrants and missionaries began during these years to win some converts among blacks, as did representatives of the Baha'i faith.

Blacks who affiliated with such groups were a small minority during this period, yet they shared in a larger pattern of growing African-American identification with peoples of color internationally. Black Americans tended to look with favor on the rise of Japan, a powerful modern nation-state not controlled by whites. Toyohiko Kagawa (1888–1960), on a speaking tour of the United States in 1936, was praised by Francis Grimké as the leading Christian of his age, while a year later the noted black leader W. E. B. Du Bois (1868–1963), just back from a tour of East Asia, regretted that African Americans had not done with Haitian Vodou what he thought the Japanese had done with Shinto: turn an ancient myth into a modernizing ideology. There was also considerable African-American interest in Gandhi, long before nonviolent resistance became the established strategy of the early civil rights movement. Prominent African-American leaders who called on him in India in the 1930s included Benjamin Mays (1895–1984), Howard Thurman (1900–1981), and Sue Bailey Thurman (1903–1996). Howard Thurman's eclectic mysticism and his pastorate of the Church of All Peoples in San Francisco, a congregation both interracial and interreligious, is a further mark of this tendency to forge global religious ties. So too is Benjamin Mays's notable participation, through the YMCA, the Federal Council, and the World Council of Churches, in the international world of ecumenical Protestantism, where, especially under the prodding of the missionary movement, the struggle against racial injustice was an increasingly prominent concern. At the same time, African Americans in the United States increasingly found allies, even in the southern states, in their struggle to overturn the legacy of slavery and segregation. The Southern Tenant Farmers' Union of the 1930s and 1940s, which enjoyed national support from secular and religious radicals but depended on black church leadership at the grass roots, in many ways anticipated the later civil rights movement. In the post–World War II era, Cold War concerns that racial discrimination at home undercut the struggle with Communism abroad gave further impetus to racial reform.

The career of Martin Luther King, Jr., represented at once the culmination and frustration of these tendencies. Like such figures as Mays and Thurman, King in his theological orientation was more in tune with the immanentalism of the older Modernism than with Neo-Orthodoxy, and his direct action tactics, though confrontational, were more in line with the harmonialism of the Social Gospel than the Christian realism of Reinhold Niebuhr. His defense of Gandhian nonviolence, especially in the face of a rising critique from Malcolm X (Malcolm Little, later El-Hajj Malik El-Shabazz; 1925–1965), onetime spokesman for the Nation of Islam and, at the end of his life, a more traditional Muslim, mixed with tactical considerations a deep affirmation of the conciliatory and community-creating power of God.

The Crises of the 1960s

Recent scholarship has given varying weight to the centrality of African-American Christianity in the civil rights movement, which in two landmark laws passed by the United States Congress in 1964 and 1965 won an end to legal patterns of discrimination in public accommodations and the effective denial of the franchise to most blacks in the South. Some have argued that the movement was decisively religious, that it was institutionally based in the black churches, led by black preachers, and defined by a black Christian ethos, evident above all in its music. Others have noted the hesitant support of many local black churches and the outright resistance to King by some black Protestant establishment leaders, above all the powerful Joseph H. Jackson (1900–1990) of the National Baptist Convention, U.S.A. They have contended that the cutting edge of the movement was always to be found among secular radicals, who found in the black churches an important recruiting ground, but were not in the end constrained by a Christian ethos or commitment to nonviolence, as is evident from the eruption of the Black Power movement, which combined elements of an older black nationalism with the anticolonial radicalism articulated by such figures as Frantz Fanon (1925–1961). In the Black Theology movement, associated above all with the writings of James H. Cone (1938–), African-American Christianity sought to absorb the Black Power critique and eventually to forge a coalition with the other "liberation theologies" emerging in Africa, Latin America, and Asia, as well as among African-American women, who adopted the term "womanist" to distinguish themselves from white feminists. In articulating his initial position, Cone drew more on Sartre and Continental Neo-

Orthodoxy than on the older liberalism, and his theology emphasized enduring conflict, not cosmic harmony.

The churches of the Protestant establishment, which had taken
unprecedented steps to support King and the civil rights movement, were stunned by the eruption in their own midst of the Black
Power movement, evident not only in Black Theology, but in separatist black caucuses in many denominations and above all by the
Black Manifesto movement of the late 1960s, which demanded the
churches pay substantial reparations for past racism. This critical
moment in the encounter of blacks and whites in the United States,
both within and beyond the churches, coincided with and greatly
intensified parallel crises in the articulation of American national
purpose and the definition of American diversity. Writing in the
early 1960s, the sociologist Robert Bellah (1927–) had advanced
the concept of American "civil religion" not only to describe an independent zone of public religion in clear differentiation from the
churches, but to defend the authenticity of religious reflection on
American destiny not defined by the Christian tradition. In spite
of Bellah's subsequent effort to insist that such reflection could be
deeply critical, there was in the context of the late 1960s widespread
reaction against all religiously based affirmations of America's special mission. Especially in the most radical wing of the growing
movement of opposition to the war in Vietnam, the global power
of the United States was increasingly attacked as the chief bulwark
of racial and class oppression, which American religion too much
had legitimated. Such criticisms were also increasingly heard within
the churches, where in mainstream Protestantism both a left-leaning
pacifism and a revival of just war theory increasingly challenged
Niebuhrian realism, while American Catholicism produced in the
Berrigan brothers, Daniel (1921–) and Phillip (1924–2002), antiwar
activists whose illegal protests led to their conviction and imprison-
ment. A rising ecological movement attacked both industrial civilization and the traditions of western religion claimed to have promoted it. A fascination with Zen Buddhism, which had slowly grown

in literary and liberal religious circles over the twentieth century, now flowered into a widening interest in Asian religious ideas and practices, both within and beyond the churches. Thomas Merton (1915–1968), the Trappist monk whose writings in the aftermath of World War II had exemplified the turn to tradition, now appeared as an agent of increasing dialogue with the East, and as part of a new Catholicism committed to peace, racial justice, and the reforms of Vatican II. Within academic theology, meanwhile, a sharp turn away from Neo-Orthodoxy led to a revival of the modernist impulse, which quickly passed through the cheerful secularization theology of the early Harvey Cox (1929–) to a more unsettling critique of the western religious tradition generally. The broader cultural ramifications of this were signaled in April 1966 when *Time*, a leading mass-circulation magazine, grouping into a movement a disparate collection of Protestant and Jewish theologians, Thomas Altizer (1927–), William Hamilton (1924–), Paul Van Buren (1924–1998), and Richard Rubenstein (1924–), blazoned on its cover the question: "Is God Dead?" Such radical questioning, along with more moderate critiques, emerged as well from a reinvigorated feminist movement, which now appeared with ever increasing force across the whole spectrum of American religious life. The way in which feminist thought could begin within the churches but then move entirely beyond them is most strikingly evident in the career of onetime Catholic lay theologian Mary Daly (1928–). Meanwhile, the rising assertion of an oppositional identity among black Americans helped promote a parallel rejection of assimilationism among American Jews, who at the same time found their past political alliance with African Americans complicated by the politics of affirmative action, black radical critiques of Israel, and the growing influence of Islam. Though its gravity was not understood at the time, a major modification of American immigration law in 1965, which overturned the quota system of 1924, quietly set in motion a deep process of change in the racial, ethnic, and religious character of the nation's population.

A Changing Balance of Power among Protestants

In the midst of all this, the core denominations of the older Protestantism in the United States, the major bearers (in however altered form) of the Reformed tradition so influential from the nation's founding, entered a time of unprecedented institutional crisis
and decline and were less and less able either to command the center
of American religious life or to put their stamp on American Protestantism as a whole. Membership declined both in absolute terms and
in comparison with other Protestant groups—as was already clear by
the mid-1980s. By 1985, such churches as the Episcopal Church, the
United Church of Christ, and the United Methodist Church had fif-
teen to twenty percent fewer members than they had reported in
1965. Such losses have not been recovered subsequently. Meanwhile,
the conservative evangelical and even more the Holiness and Pentecostal churches continued to grow, sometimes spectacularly. In 1965,
the Southern Baptist Convention, with just under eleven million
members, was slightly smaller than the Methodists, but two decades
later, having grown to fourteen and a half million, it was over fifty
percent larger than the shrinking United Methodist Church and
undisputedly the largest Protestant denomination in the United
States. The Assemblies of God reported nearly a quadrupling of its
membership during this same period, reaching the two million mark
and surpassing in size such smaller mainline churches as the Disciples of Christ and the United Church of Christ. Rapid growth persisted as well among such groups as the Seventh-Day Adventists and
the Mormons, with the Church of Jesus Christ of Latter-Day Saints
claiming over three and a half million members by the mid-1980s.

These more rapidly growing bodies have not only increasingly
surpassed mainstream Protestantism in numbers, they have also
provided the political constituency for a rival Protestant attempt to
shape American public life. The churches of the old Protestant establishment have largely accommodated themselves to trends arising in
the 1960s, albeit to various degrees, with more enthusiasm among

officialdom and the clergy than among the laity, and in some cases only against serious and continuing internal resistance. Considerable questioning of the overseas use of American military power has persisted, as has support for the greater inclusion of blacks and other minorities in both church and society. Theological education is generally marked by the significant influence of feminist theology and women faculty, and women constitute a steadily increasing percentage of the ordained clergy. Changed views regarding sexuality and gender have included increased acceptance of homosexuality, though the issue of gay ordination has been hotly contested, most notably among the Presbyterians. (After the election of V. Gene Robinson, a gay priest, to the bishopric in 2003, the divisions on this question threatened not only to divide the Episcopal Church in the United States, but to split up the Worldwide Anglican Communion.) A tolerant openness to non-Christian forms of religious belief and practice and a concurrent disinterest in sustaining the conversion-oriented missionary enterprise of a former day are part of an increasingly eclectic ethos. Conservative evangelicals, Pentecostals, and other Protestants outside the old mainstream, albeit with many exceptions and variations, have generally taken opposing positions, seeing in the legacy of the 1960s a fundamental threat to America's religious and social well-being. They are now the main supporters of overseas missions and some among them have mounted an extended campaign at home against what they consider the inroads of "secular humanism," evident most especially in the public schools, where a 1962 Supreme Court decision, *Engel v. Vitale*, banned school prayer and began the erosion of Protestantism's de facto control of the American public school system. They have also in recent decades provided support for episodically successful campaigns to require the teaching of "creation science" alongside evolution. Though scarcely untouched by feminism or lacking in women leaders, they were critically important in the defeat of the Equal Rights Amendment to the constitution and have strongly opposed the practice of abortion and labored to reverse *Roe v. Wade*, the United States Supreme Court decision of 1973 that rendered it legal. They have resisted the gay/lesbian rights movement. They tend to be more supportive of the exercise of American power abroad and of free market capitalism at home. Though their ranks include those sectors of American Protestantism historically most active in the defense of racial segregation, they have in various ways moved toward more inclusionary ideas and practices, Mormonism's abandonment in 1978 of its exclusion of blacks from ordination to the priesthood (otherwise open to all young males) being only one example of a much larger trend. The determination of conservative Protestants to maintain firm control over their own institutional base is strikingly evident in the Southern Baptist Convention, where Fundamentalists and conservative evangelicals in the last quarter of the twentieth century tightened their grip and dislodged most liberals from any positions of power.

The ability of more conservative Protestants to press their agenda nationally in recent decades has been decisively shaped by political realignments rooted in the events of the 1960s. Northern Protestants have been predominately affiliated with the Republican Party since its origins, and even among the older mainline denominations such an affiliation persists, albeit in attenuated form. The end of segregation in the South brought newly enfranchised black voters into the Democratic Party, with a concurrent shift of many whites, largely evangelical Protestants, to the Republican Party. The candidacy of "born-again" though liberal Southern Baptist Jimmy Carter (1924–; president, 1977–1981) enabled the Democrats to recover some of these defectors in 1976, celebrated in the media as "the year of the evangelical," but this was merely a temporary phenomenon. For the first time since the antebellum period, northern and southern evangelical Protestants came overwhelmingly to share the same partisan loyalties and soon emerged as a powerful force within the Republican Party. The Moral Majority, led by Jerry Falwell (1933–), a preacher in the Baptist Bible Fellowship, a Fundamentalist group, was highly visible in the campaign of 1980, which elected Ronald Reagan (1911–2004; president, 1981–1989) to the presidency, though its actual organizational strength was much less than many

commentators of the time imagined. Much stronger at the grassroots
level was the Christian Coalition, organized in 1989 by Marion (Pat)
Robertson (1930–), a Baptist minister, television talk-show host, and
charismatic, who had run unsuccessfully for the Republican presidential nomination in 1988. Particularly notable here is the growing mobilization of Pentecostals, who have become an increasingly
important component in (what is known as) the Christian Right.
Even this shared partisan loyalty and growing grassroots mobilization have not, however, allowed conservative evangelicals to promote
their vision of a morally renewed America without enlisting allies of
other traditions. Muting their historic anti-Catholicism, they have
worked to forge an alliance with conservative Catholics around such
issues as abortion, a collaboration eased by the development of a significant charismatic movement within American Catholicism. Building on their intense, if sometimes apocalyptic, support for Israel,
they have also developed ties to politically conservative Jews. Nevertheless, conservative Protestants have had only limited success in
achieving such central goals as curtailing abortion and defending the
place of religious ideas and practice in the public schools.

The Heightened Role of Catholicism in American Public Life

A divided American Protestantism is no longer inclined to achieve
unity or shape the public order through a shared opposition to
Roman Catholicism, nor is a decaying Protestant establishment any
longer able to treat American Catholics as junior partners in a triple
establishment of Protestants, Catholics, and Jews. Roman Catholicism has now moved in a new way into the center of American religious life, and taken on an unprecedented, if precarious, role in the
public realm. In many ways, it holds within itself all the conflict and
complexity that in Protestantism is divided among separate bodies. Though scarcely as monolithic in previous periods as outsiders
sometimes imagined, American Catholicism in the wake of Vatican II became in a new way an arena for public contestation, as def-

erence to ecclesiastical authority and conventional patriotism waned. American Catholics responded to *Humanae Vitae*, Pope Paul VI's (1897–1978; pope, 1963–1978) 1968 encyclical restating the long-standing prohibition against most methods of birth control, with vigorous criticism and massive noncompliance. John F. Kennedy had run for president in 1960 as, among other things, a war hero, but his brother Robert (1925–1968), like another Catholic, Eugene McCarthy (1916–), sought the Democratic nomination in 1968 on an anti–Vietnam War platform. Increasingly, over the later decades of the twentieth century, the American Catholic electorate tended to be more or less evenly divided between the major parties, and small shifts in its allegiance could have large electoral consequences. With evangelical Protestants seeking to recruit conservative Catholics to their new "moral majority," and liberal Protestants drawing heavily on Latin American liberation theology in their opposition to United States' support for anti-Sandinista forces in Nicaragua, Catholics were visibly present on both sides of the political battles and "culture wars" of the 1980s and thereafter. At the same time, American Catholic bishops often sought to define a middle ground, more conservative on issues of reproduction, sexuality, and gender, but more liberal on questions of economic justice and international relations. When the National Conference of Catholic Bishops in 1983 issued "The Challenge of Peace," its carefully nuanced and much-discussed pastoral letter on nuclear weapons, the Catholic bishops seemed to have taken up the role of the old Protestant establishment in judiciously articulating a common standard of morality, but when Archbishop John O'Connor (1920–2000) of New York in 1984 chastised Democratic vice presidential candidate Geraldine Ferraro, a Catholic, for not actively promoting the church's position on abortion, he raised old fears about Catholicism's role in American politics. Though the presence of a vigorous feminist movement within Roman Catholicism has altered the picture considerably, the church's teachings on abortion and refusal to ordain women to the priesthood still fuel an anti-Catholicism centered on the status of women. The difficulty of maintaining central ground was vividly evident in the crisis, beginning in 2002, over sexual abuse by the clergy, as the bishops were caught between liberals attacking sexual harassment and an abuse of power and conservatives decrying the presence of homosexuals among the clergy. Assertions of the need for more lay influence in such matters, echoing localistic tendencies reaching all the way back to early nineteenth-century "trusteeism," also challenged the Vatican's promotion of increased hierarchical control of the American church. Meanwhile, though immigration has helped Catholicism, which now counts more than a fifth of the population among its adherents, to maintain its numerical strength, decades of decline in the number of candidates for ordination and membership in religious orders raise questions of Roman Catholicism's long-term institutional strength in the United States.

Changes in African-American Christianity and the Growing Importance of Islam

In the competition among religious groups to shape the public order in America, African-American Christianity stands at the other end of the political spectrum from the Christian Right of conservative white Protestantism, even though their shared connection in past traditions of American evangelicalism provides an important point of contact. With blacks remaining as overwhelmingly attached to the Democratic Party as white evangelicals and Pentecostals now are to the Republicans, and with the enfranchisement of the southern black population after 1965, much of the energy the black churches previously invested in the civil rights movement was channeled into electoral politics. The campaigns of former civil rights activist and Baptist clergyman Jesse Jackson (1941–) to secure the Democratic Party's nomination in 1984 and 1988 are only the most obvious examples of a broader trend. Jackson's success in mobilizing the black electorate indicates the continuing strength of the older black Protestant establishment in African-American life, even as his attempts to build an inclusive "Rainbow Coalition" around a broadly left-oriented political agenda aimed to harness growing American diversity to a vision of the American common good consistent with that of Martin Luther King, Jr. Nevertheless, increasing diversity has challenged the power of black as well as white mainstream Protestantism in ways that sometimes complicate the task of building religiously based movements within the black community and creating coalitions beyond it. Within the ever more diverse realm of black Christianity, the Baptists no longer enjoy the clear preeminence they held through the twentieth century. Most notably, Holiness and Pentecostal churches have grown with great rapidity. Leaders from this sector of the black churches seem somewhat more inclined than the older leadership to forge alliances with conservatives on such issues as the use of public funds, channeled through vouchers to parents, to support children's attendance at private religious schools. Though the wave of black conversions to Catholicism subsided after the mid-1970s, immigration has subsequently enlarged the numbers of African-American Catholics. Outside the churches, the most important development in African-American religious life is the growing and increasingly varied presence of Islam. With the death of Elijah Muhammad in 1975, the Nation of Islam, under the leadership of his son Wallace Deen Muhammad (who later took the name Warithuddin Muhammad, 1933–), abandoned most of its distinctive teachings, embraced more orthodox patterns of Sunni Islam, passed through a series of name changes, and eventually evolved into the more loosely organized Society of American Muslims. W. Deen Muhammad, apparently in an effort further to link African-American Muslims with immigrant Islam, resigned from the leadership of even this group in 2003. This development is consistent with the dominant tendency of African-American Muslims increasingly to attach themselves to the growing Islamic community in the United States rather than perpetuate the distinctive forms of Islam emerging among North American blacks earlier in the century. The major significant countervailing tendency has been the revived Nation of Islam, formed by Louis Farrakhan (Louis Eugene Wolcott, 1933–) to perpetuate the teachings of Elijah Muhammad after the old Nation had abandoned them, and even Farrakhan's group moved closer to the Muslim mainstream toward the century's end. Farrakhan's active support of Jesse Jackson in 1984 helped mobilize African Americans, but impaired Jackson's standing with Jews. In organizing the 1995 Million Man March on Washington, D.C., Farrakhan also succeeded in attracting both considerable grassroots support and vigorous criticism, in part because of the Nation of Islam's firm traditionalism on questions of sexuality and gender roles.

Change and Continuity

In his survey history of American religion published in the early 1970s, Sydney Ahlstrom (1919–1984) declared that the Puritan Epoch, a four-hundred-year period in Anglo-American history that coincided with the Tridentine era in the history of Roman Catholicism, had ended in the 1960s. His thesis still has merit, as does his related assertion that African-American religious history would be paradigmatic for a reinterpretation of the continuing history of American Christianity. Whatever ended in the 1960s, however, it does not seem to have resulted either in the triumph of secularization or the decline of religion in some general sense. Recent scholarship has made the claim that adherence to religious bodies has advanced more or less steadily throughout American history, even into the late twentieth century. Increasing emphasis has also been placed on the continuities between Protestantism's more recent and its earlier history in America. Claims that mainline Protestants are newly afflicted with a taste for New Age piety and a do-it-yourself eclecticism have been qualified by attention to the persistent strand of harmonialism that runs from Transcendentalism through such earlier twentieth-century figures as Glenn Clark (1882–1956), E. Stanley Jones (1884–1973), and Norman Vincent Peale (1898–1993). The current prominence of women in the denominations of the old Protestant establishment also clearly has its roots in nineteenth-century evangelicalism. The late twentieth-century decline in older more "respectable" groups and rapid growth of newer denominations has been compared to developments in the early national period, when Episcopalians, Congregationalists, and Presbyterians were first eclipsed, most especially by Baptists and Methodists. The recent history of Catholicism in the United States also echoes many earlier themes, and if post–Vatican II "cafeteria Catholics" seem more like liberal Protestants than traditional Catholics, it is worth remembering that the standardization of Catholic practice has always been more an aim of the hierarchy than a routine habit of the laity. While the use of explicitly Christian discourse in the public realm has occasioned sharp criticism in recent decades, it has scarcely disappeared, but seems rather to have increased. For American Christianity, the deepest transition that the 1960s marked may in the long run prove to be the turn to a deepening globalization, a decisive turn away from the period in which Christianity was so closely tied to European descent. Here too, of course, new departures have their roots in old patterns, above all those associated with the history of African-American Christianity in the United States.

Globalization

American churches' deepening involvement in the emergence of a truly global Christianity is evident on one side by their ever-increasing involvement in international missions. Though the churches of the old Protestant mainstream no longer deploy the worldwide missionary presence they once did, their members are still quietly present in the overseas work of many government agencies and nongovernmental voluntary associations. American Catholics, working through many religious orders, as well as the Maryknoll Catholic Foreign Missionary Society of America, organized by the American Catholic bishops in 1911, also constitute an ongoing link to Catholic life outside the United States. Most striking in the late twentieth century, however, was the growing overseas presence of the same Protestant movements and churches that are most rapidly growing in the United States. Billy Graham (1918–), who emerged at midcentury as the most prominent Protestant evangelist since the death of Dwight L. Moody (1837–1899) and who remained for fifty years a widely influential leader among American evangelicals, took his revivalistic "crusades" far beyond the borders not only of the United States but of English-speaking evangelicalism more generally. He also helped promote a series of international conferences intended to renew the drive for worldwide evangelization. Alongside such conservative evangelical efforts, there has also been a growth in Holiness and Pentecostal missions, as well as those of such groups as the Seventh-Day Adventists, the Jehovah's Witnesses, and the Mormons. Often thought of in the past as distinctively and indigenously American, these latter groups have now become truly international. Mormon membership increased tenfold between 1950 and 2000, and while the overwhelming majority of Mormons at midcentury were Americans, by the century's end most lived outside the United States and many did not speak English. Generally, these missionary efforts have wholeheartedly embraced the emphasis on winning converts that the older mainstream missions generally abandoned, and often they have just as assiduously avoided the social justice issues the older missions increasingly came to emphasize. Nevertheless, within these circles, sometimes under the pressure of indigenous leadership, movements toward a more balanced approach have appeared. It is noteworthy that at the Berlin Conference of 1968, an early American-led attempt to reinvigorate evangelical missions, it was black delegates who challenged the body to emulate rather than merely invoke the social reformism of early evangelicalism.

Within the United States itself, increasing globalization must be defined primarily with regard to immigration. Since 1965, legal immigration to the United States has sharply increased, reaching and on occasion exceeding the very high levels of the period immediately before World War I. During this same period, there has also been very substantial illegal immigration. By 2000, more than thirty-one million of the United States' two hundred eighty-one million people, more than one in ten, were foreign-born. This was an increase of eleven and one-third million over 1990. The origins of the immigrant population have also dramatically shifted. In 1900, eighty-five percent of the roughly ten million foreign-born people in America came from Europe. By 1990, Europeans represented less than one-quarter of the foreign-born in the United States. In the early 1990s, for every newcomer from Europe, there were two from Asia (in its broadest definition) and nearly four from elsewhere in the Americas—the largest number of these coming from Mexico, but with a strong representation from the Caribbean also, as well as significant numbers from Central and South America. The number of African immigrants is considerably smaller, roughly one-fifth of the European, yet is unprecedented since the close of the slave trade. In California, in many respects the site where major American cultural and political developments first take clear shape, the day when a majority of the population descended solely from European ancestors is drawing to a close.

For Christianity in America, this immigration has two clear consequences, which are related and sometimes closely intertwined, yet nonetheless distinct. Though sometimes less remarked upon than its significance deserves, this migration is refashioning Christianity in the United States away from its European past and toward its global future, when it will increasingly draw its membership from peoples of color. Latino/a immigration is the most obvious bearer of this transformation, affecting not only Roman Catholicism but increasingly Protestantism as well, most especially conservative evangelicalism and Pentecostalism. Cuban Americans who have brought Santería and Haitian Americans who have brought Vodou to the United States have helped enlarge American religion beyond Christianity by adding to the mix religious beliefs and practices grounded in the traditional religions of Africa. At the same time, since these traditions have long histories of interconnection with Catholic beliefs and practices, they have also enriched and complicated the world of American Catholicism. Many Christians are also to be found among Asian immigrants to the United States. Vietnamese Catholics, like Latino/a Catholics, are bearers of forms of popular devotion, above all Marian devotion, that had faded among European-American Catholics since the reforms of the Second Vatican Council. Korean immigrants to the United States are overwhelmingly Christian, with an especially substantial number of Presbyterians. (The Unification Church of Sun Myung Moon [1920–], which has been compared to Mormonism both in its departure from Christian tradition and the hostility it has aroused, has only a small American membership and is not at all typical of the Korean impact on American Christianity.) This immigration has made possible within American Christianity the kind of coalition of persons of color from time to time hoped for among African Americans, but the reality has not matched the dream. Asian Americans and African Americans, both within and outside the churches, have an as yet unresolved relationship. Latino/a spokespersons sometimes claim that Latin Americans are free of the racial obsessions afflicting the United States, and will deliver the nation from its black-white problems, but there is a good deal of romanticization of Latin American racial practices in such claims. African Americans and West Indians have a long history of both conflict and collaboration, both of which tendencies are played out in religious institutions. Within the ranks of Christians of color in America, the process of framing a normative concept of pluralism has yet to run its course.

At the same time, this immigration is making present within the United States, in unprecedented numbers and vitality, the wide spectrum of human religious life that stands outside Christianity, or Judaism. While Confucianism and Taoism are increasingly part of the new religious landscape, Hinduism, Buddhism, and most especially Islam are the most significant parts of it. All of these traditions include, in varying degrees, immigrants and their descendants as well as converts won in America. Their ideas and practices are also of increasing interest to some Christians, even as their growing presence remains alarming to others. Clearly, reckoning with these new religious neighbors will be a major force in shaping the future history of Christianity in the United States. This seems above all true of its reckoning with Islam.

The growing presence of Islam in America, developing concurrently with the deepening engagement of the United States with the Islamic world overseas, in many ways raises for all American Christians issues parallel to those raised for American Protestants of an earlier period by the presence of Catholicism. International Catholicism was feared as an international force with universal aspirations, whose American adherents were unreliable in their loyalty to American democracy and to the practice of religious freedom. Parallel fears surround Islam and American Muslims. Catholicism was attacked as reactionary in its attitude toward women. So too is Islam. In its wars with Mexico and Spain in the nineteenth century, the United States fought Catholic powers, while in the Gulf War and the wars in Afghanistan and Iraq, it has engaged Islamic adversaries. It is easy to imagine that as American Protestants once forged an elusive unity and worked toward common goals in opposition to Catholics, American Christians—and Jews—might seek to build a working consensus by shared resistance to Islam. At the same time, one expects that as Muslims work their way ever more deeply into American life and, like American Catholics, adapt in a myriad of ways to its prevailing institutions and practices, the Islamic presence in America will become, as in part it already has, increasingly a matter-of-fact reality. Much will depend on the course of immigration and the developing nature of American Islamic leadership, both within the United States and within the world of Islam internationally. As among the early Catholic Americanists, one finds within Islam in the United States voices asserting the consistency of American institutions with the Qur'an and Islamic tradition, but this development seems so far in its early stages—as does the whole unfolding story of American Islam.

In the coming century, the engagement of an increasingly globalized Christianity with the growing presence in America of the equally global religion of Islam will test the boundaries of acceptable religious pluralism and deeply shape the definition of the common good and national purpose in the United States. It may also profoundly affect the encounter of black and white in America. A profound difference between the historic place of Catholicism in America and the developing role of Islam lies just at this point. Though Islam is sometimes embraced by African Americans, much as Roman Catholicism has been at times, as a universal community that transcends the particularities of race embedded in Protestantism, the affirmation of Islamic identity has also had for African Americans an oppositional potential beyond that typical of Catholicism. The ability of the Nation of Islam to give such powerful voice to black alienation in the United States has rested in part precisely on its rejection of Christianity as a "white man's religion," a potential shared by other forms of Islam as well. African-American Christians have both vigorously disputed and partially embraced this critique. Islam's claim to be freer from racism than Christianity has also been challenged. In the future encounter, within the United States, of global Christianity with global Islam, their engagement with the realities of race will be a central part of the story.

A Note on Contemporary Membership Statistics

Reliable and standardized figures for the membership of various Christian denominations and other religious bodies in the United States are very difficult, even impossible, to obtain. The United States Census Bureau does not include questions about religion in its decennial surveys of the American population. The National Council of Churches of Christ in the United States of America publishes an annual *Yearbook of American and Canadian Churches,* which contains membership figures for most if not all Christian bodies in the United States. These figures are self-reported. Some groups regularly update their reports, some do not. Some base their reports on meticulous record keeping, some submit very rough estimates. Some provide "inclusive membership" figures that are much higher than those for "full communicant or confirmed members," others provide only a single set of figures. Independent studies of particular churches or groups of churches sometimes produce figures quite different from those reported by the organizations themselves. Both within and even more outside the churches, highly varied results appear depending on whether figures are based on membership in specific religious organizations or the size of a particular ethnic constituency that a particular set of religious bodies are thought to serve. Studies based not on membership reports, but on survey data are subject to all the standard controversies about the adequacy of the sample used, the appropriateness of the questions asked, and the interpretation of the data gathered. Disagreement about the size of various religious groups is also a matter of public contestation, as partisans claim various constituencies are being exaggerated or minimized unfairly.

It is clear that there are very high levels of affiliation with Christian churches in the United States. The United States Census of 2000 reported a total population of 281.4 million, while the closest equivalent *Yearbook* figures claim an inclusive church membership of 152.1 million. Recent survey research, in which people are asked to identify their religious identity, reports that roughly 75 to 80 percent of the United States population identify themselves as Christian.

The largest single group of Christians in the United States is by far the Roman Catholic Church, reporting an inclusive membership of 62 million. This figure alone makes clear the current central place of Catholicism in American religious life. In recent surveys of religious self-identification, around one-quarter of all Americans usually indicate they are Roman Catholics.

Around fifty to fifty-five percent of Americans identify themselves as Protestants, but these are divided among many traditions and denominations. There are some significant discrepancies between membership figures reported by the denominations and patterns of self-identification reported by survey research. Denominational figures for Pentecostal groups, for example, are not matched by survey research. Different portraits also appear depending on whether one groups all related denominations into "families" or considers each denomination individually. One recent survey has estimated the constituency for various denominational families as follows: Baptist 33.8 million, Methodist/Wesleyan 14.1 million, Lutheran 9.6 million, Presbyterian 5.6 million, Pentecostal/Charismatic 4.4 million, Episcopal/Anglican 3.5 million, Latter-Day Saints 2.7 million, Churches of Christ 2.6 million, Congregational/United Church of Christ 1.4 million, Jehovah's Witnesses 1.3 million, and Assemblies of God 1.1 million. This estimate may be compared to the membership figures published in the *Yearbook*. The largest Protestant body is the Southern Baptist Convention at 16 million. The next largest body, the United Methodist Church, claims 8.3 million, but some observers believe this is an overly scrupulous report that understates the denomination's constituency by nearly 3 million. The National Baptist Convention, U.S.A., had in the 1990s claimed to be of comparable size to the United Methodists, but its report of 8.2 million members has been challenged and until a new count is completed it is not listed in the *Yearbook*. Three denominations fall around the 5 million mark. The Church of God in Christ has since the early 1990s claimed 5.5 million members, but other reports suggest a membership under 5 million. The Church of Jesus Christ of Latter-Day Saints reports an inclusive membership of 5.2 million, while the Evangelical Lutheran Church in America claims an inclusive membership of 5.1 million. Two churches may fall in the 3 to 4 million range. The Presbyterian Church (U.S.A.) claims an inclusive membership of 3.5 million, as does the National Baptist Convention of America, but the latter number has been challenged. The remaining groups that claim, with varying degrees of reliability, a million members or more are as follows: Assemblies of God 2.6 million, Lutheran Church–Missouri Synod 2.6 million, African Methodist Episcopal Church 2.5 million, National Missionary Baptist Convention of America 2.5 million, Progressive National Baptist Convention 2.5 million, Episcopal Church 2.3 million, Churches of Christ 1.5 million, Pentecostal Assemblies of the World 1.5 million, American Baptist Churches in the USA 1.4 million, United Church of Christ 1.4 million, African Methodist Episcopal Zion Church 1.3 million, Baptist Bible Fellowship International 1.2 million, Christian Churches and Churches of Christ 1.1 million, and Jehovah's Witnesses 1 million. There are also many denominations with a reported membership of less than 1 million.

The two largest Orthodox bodies, the Greek Orthodox Archdiocese of North America and the Orthodox Church in America, have reported inclusive memberships of 1.5 and 1 million respectively, but a recent study suggests their adherents number 440,000 and 115,000 only. Recent survey research indicates that around 1 percent of the American population identifies itself as Orthodox.

Beyond the churches, membership counts are, if anything, more disputed, in part because of the very heavy reliance on survey data and disagreements about whether such studies adequately represent the most recent and economically marginal immigrants. Much controversy surrounds the question of whether Islam has surpassed Judaism as America's second largest faith. Current estimates of the Jewish population range from 5.5 to 7.7 million members, the higher number including all persons of Jewish origin. Of these, perhaps 2.4 to 3 million identify explicitly with Judaism. Estimates of the Muslim population in the United States around the year 2000 have run as high as 6 to 8 million and as low as 500,000, with the more plausible estimates falling in the 2 to 4 million range. Estimates of the number of Buddhists run from around 1.4 to 2.3 million, while Hindus are thought to number between 850,000 and 1.1 million.

Bibliography

General

Ahlstrom, Sydney E. *A Religious History of the American People.* New Haven, Conn.: Yale University Press, 1972.

Bacon, Leonard Woolsey. *A History of American Christianity.* American Church History Series 13. New York: Christian Literature, 1897.

Baird, Robert. *Religion in America; or, An Account of the Origin, Progress, Relation to the State, and Present Condition of the Evangelical Churches in the United States.* New York: Harper, 1844.

Bowden, Henry Warner. *American Indians and Christian Missions: Studies in Cultural Conflict.* Chicago: University of Chicago Press, 1981.

Burr, Nelson R. *A Critical Bibliography of Religion in America.* Princeton, N.J.: Princeton University Press, 1961.

Davis, Cyprian. *The History of Black Catholics in the United States.* New York: Crossroad, 1990.

Dictionary of Christianity in America. Edited by Daniel G. Reid. Downers Grove, Ill.: InterVarsity, 1990.

Dolan, Jay P. *The American Catholic Experience: A History from Colonial Times to the Present.* Garden City, N.Y.: Doubleday, 1985.

Dorchester, Daniel. *Christianity in the United States from the First Settlement Down to the Present Time.* New York: Hunt & Eaton, 1885.

Encyclopedia of Religion in the South. Edited by Samuel S. Hill. Macon, Ga.: Mercer University Press, 1984.

Encyclopedia of the American Religious Experience: Studies of Traditions and Movements. Edited by Charles H. Lippy and Peter W. Williams. New York: Scribner, 1988.

Finke, Roger, and Rodney Stark. *The Churching of America, 1776–1990: Winners and Losers in Our Religious Economy.* New Brunswick, N.J.: Rutgers University Press, 1992.

Fulop, Timothy E., and Albert J. Raboteau, eds. *African-American Religion: Interpretive Essays in History and Culture.* New York: Routledge, 1997.

Hall, David D., ed. *Lived Religion in America: Toward a History of Practice in America.* Princeton, N.J.: Princeton University Press, 1997.

Hennesey, James. *American Catholics: A History of the Roman Catholic Community in the United States.* New York: Oxford University Press, 1981.

Hertzberg, Arthur. *The Jews in America: Four Centuries of an Uneasy Encounter; A History.* New York: Simon & Schuster, 1988.

Hutchison, William R. *Errand to the World: American Protestant Thought and Foreign Missions.* Chicago: University of Chicago Press, 1987.

———. *Religious Pluralism in America: The Contentious History of a Founding Ideal.* New Haven, Conn.: Yale University Press, 2003.

Marsden, George M. *The Soul of the American University: From Protestant Establishment to Established Nonbelief.* New York: Oxford University Press, 1994.

Marty, Marty E. "American Religious History in the Eighties: A Decade of Achievement." *Church History* 62 (1993): 335–77.

Mead, Frank Spencer. *Handbook of Denominations in the United States.* New York: Abingdon, 1951. Several subsequent editions, revised by Samuel S. Hill, and later Craig D. Atwood.

Mead, Sidney E. *The Lively Experiment: The Shaping of Christianity in America.* New York: Harper & Row, 1963.

———. *The Nation with the Soul of a Church.* New York: Harper & Row, 1975.

Moore, R. Laurence. *Religious Outsiders and the Making of Americans.* New York: Oxford University Press, 1986.

———. *Selling God: American Religion in the Marketplace of Culture.* New York: Oxford University Press, 1994.

Mullin, Bruce, and Russell E. Richey, eds. *Reimagining Denominationalism: Interpretive Essays.* New York: Oxford University Press, 1994.

Noll, Mark A. *The Old Religion in a New World: The History of North American Christianity.* Grand Rapids, Mich.: Eerdmans, 2002.

Raboteau, Albert J. *Canaan Land: A Religious History of African Americans.* New York: Oxford University Press, 2001.

Raboteau, Albert J., David W. Wills, Randall K. Burkett, Will B. Gravely, and James M. Washington. "Retelling Carter Woodson's Story. Archival Sources for Afro-American Church History." *Journal of American History* 77 (1990): 183–99.

Robert, Dana Lee. *American Women in Mission: A Social History of Their Thought and Practice.* Macon, Ga.: Mercer University Press, 1996.

Schaff, Philip. *America: A Sketch of Its Political, Social, and Religious Character* [1855]. Edited by Perry Miller. Cambridge, Mass.: Harvard University Press, 1961.

Stein, Stephen J. "'Something Old, Something New, Something Borrowed, Something Left to Do': Choosing a Textbook for Religion in America." *Religion and American Culture* 3 (1993): 217–27.

Stout, Harry S., and D. G. Hart, eds. *New Directions in American Religious History.* New York: Oxford University Press, 1997.

Sweet, William Warren. *The Story of Religions in America.* New York: Harper, 1930. 2d rev. ed., 1950.

Tweed, Thomas A., ed. *Retelling U.S. Religious History.* Berkeley: University of California Press, 1997.

Weisenfeld, Judith, and Richard Newman, eds. *This Far by Faith: Readings in African-American Women's Religious Biography.* New York: Routledge, 1996.

Williams, Peter W., ed. *Perspectives on American Religion and Culture.* Malden, Mass.: Blackwell, 1999.

Woodson, Carter G. *The History of the Negro Church.* Washington, D.C.: Associated Publishers, 1921.

Colonies in the Atlantic World

Butler, Jon. *Awash in a Sea of Faith: Christianizing the American People.* Cambridge, Mass.: Harvard University Press, 1990.

Davis, David Brion. *The Problem of Slavery in Western Culture.* Ithaca, N.Y.: Cornell University Press, 1966.

———. *The Problem of Slavery in the Age of the Revolution, 1770–1823.* Ithaca, N.Y.: Cornell University Press, 1975.

Fiering, Norman. *Moral Philosophy at Seventeenth-Century Harvard: A Discipline in Transition.* Chapel Hill: University of North Carolina Press, 1981.

———. *Jonathan Edwards's Moral Thought and Its British Context.* Chapel Hill: University of North Carolina Press, 1981.

Frey, Sylvia R., and Betty Wood. *Come Shouting to Zion: African American Protestantism in the American South and British Caribbean to 1830.* Chapel Hill: University of North Carolina Press, 1998.

Gaustad, Edwin S. *Sworn on the Altar of God: A Religious Biography of Thomas Jefferson.* Grand Rapids, Mich.: Eerdmans, 1996.

Gutiérrez, Ramón A. *When Jesus Came, the Corn Mothers Went Away: Marriage, Sexuality, and Power in New Mexico, 1500–1846.* Stanford, Calif.: Stanford University Press, 1991.

Hall, David D. *Worlds of Wonder, Days of Judgment: Popular Religious Belief in Early New England.* Cambridge, Mass.: Harvard University Press, 1989.

Heimert, Alan. *Religion and the American Mind, from the Great Awakening to the Revolution.* Cambridge, Mass.: Harvard University Press, 1966.

Lambert, Frank. *Inventing the "Great Awakening."* Princeton, N.J.: Princeton University Press, 1999.

Marini, Stephen A. *Radical Sects of Revolutionary New England.* Cambridge, Mass.: Harvard University Press, 1982.

Marsden, George M. *Jonathan Edwards: A Life.* New Haven, Conn.: Yale University Press, 2003.

May, Henry F. *The Enlightenment in America.* New York: Oxford University Press, 1976.

Miller, Perry. *Orthodoxy in Massachusetts, 1630–1650.* Cambridge, Mass.: Harvard University Press, 1933.

Schmidt, Leigh Eric. *Holy Fairs: Scotland and the Making of American Revivalism.* Grand Rapids, Mich.: Eerdmans, 2001.

Stout, Harry S. *The New England Soul: Preaching and Religious Culture in Colonial New England.* New York: Oxford University Press, 1986.

Weber, David J. *The Spanish Frontier in North America.* New Haven, Conn.: Yale University Press, 1992.

A Continental Nation-State

Blumhofer, Edith L. *Restoring the Faith: The Assemblies of God, Pentecostalism, and American Culture.* Urbana: University of Illinois Press, 1993.

Braude, Ann. *Radical Spirits: Spiritualism and Women's Rights in Nineteenth-Century America.* Boston: Beacon, 1989.

Breckus, Catherine A. *Strangers and Pilgrims: Female Preaching in America, 1740–1845.* Chapel Hill: University of North Carolina Press, 1998.

Brooke, John L. *The Refiner's Fire: The Making of Mormon Cosmology, 1644–1844.* New York: Cambridge University Press, 1994.

Glaude, Eddie S., Jr. *Exodus! Race, Religion, and Nation in Early Nineteenth-Century America.* Chicago: University of Chicago Press, 2000.

Harvey, Paul. *Redeeming the South: Religious Cultures and Racial Identity among Southern Baptists, 1865–1925.* Chapel Hill: University of North Carolina Press, 1997.

Hatch, Nathan O. *The Democratization of American Christianity.* New Haven, Conn.: Yale University Press, 1989.

Heyrman, Christine Leigh. *Southern Cross: The Beginnings of the Bible Belt.* New York: A. A. Knopf, 1997.

Higginbotham, Evelyn Brooks. *Righteous Discontent: The Women's Movement in the Black Baptist Church, 1880–1920.* Cambridge, Mass.: Harvard University Press, 1993.

Holifield, E. Brooks. *Theology in America: Christian Thought from the Age of the Puritans to the Civil War.* New Haven, Conn.: Yale University Press, 2003.

Hutchison, William R. *The Modernist Impulse in American Protestantism.* Cambridge, Mass.: Harvard University Press, 1976.

Luker, Ralph E. *The Social Gospel in Black and White: American Racial Reform, 1885–1912.* Chapel Hill: University of North Carolina Press, 1991.

Maffly-Kipp, Laurie F. *Religion and Society in Frontier California.* New Haven, Conn.: Yale University Press, 1994.

Marsden, George M. *Fundamentalism and American Culture: The Shaping of Twentieth-Century Evangelicalism, 1870–1925.* New York: Oxford University Press, 1980.

Noll, Mark A. *America's God: From Jonathan Edwards to Abraham Lincoln.* New York: Oxford University Press, 2002.

Raboteau, Albert J. *Slave Religion: The "Invisible Institution" in the Antebellum South*. New York: Oxford University Press, 1978.

Sanneh, Lamin. *Abolitionists Abroad: American Blacks and the Making of West Africa*. Cambridge, Mass.: Harvard University Press, 1999.

Sarna, Jonathan D., ed. *Minority Faiths and the American Protestant Mainstream*. Urbana: University of Illinois Press, 1998.

Schmidt, Leigh Eric. *Hearing Things: Religion, Illusion, and the American Enlightenment*. Cambridge, Mass.: Harvard University Press, 2000.

Seager, Richard. *The World's Parliament of Religions: The East / West Encounter*. Bloomington: Indiana University Press, 1995.

Sensbach, Jon F. *A Separate Canaan: The Making of an Afro-Moravian World in North Carolina, 1763–1840*. Chapel Hill: University of North Carolina Press, 1998.

Shipps, Jan. *Mormonism: The Story of a New Religious Tradition*. Urbana: University of Illinois Press, 1985.

Stein, Stephen J. *The Shaker Experience in America*. New Haven, Conn.: Yale University Press, 1992.

Taves, Ann. *The Household of Faith: Roman Catholic Devotions in Mid-Nineteenth-Century America*. Notre Dame, Ind.: University of Notre Dame Press, 1986.

———. *Fits, Trances, and Visions: Experiencing Religion and Explaining Experience from Wesley to James*. Princeton, N.J.: Princeton University Press, 1999.

Wacker, Grant. *Heaven Below: Early Pentecostals and American Culture*. Cambridge, Mass.: Harvard University Press, 2001.

Washington, James Melvin. *Frustrated Fellowship: The Black Baptist Quest for Social Power*. Macon, Ga.: Mercer University Press, 1986.

Wigger, John H. *Taking Heaven by Storm: Methodism and the Rise of Popular Christianity in America*. New York: Oxford University Press, 1998.

Winston, Diane H. *Red-Hot and Righteous: The Urban Religion of the Salvation Army*. Cambridge, Mass.: Harvard University Press, 1999.

A Global Power

Ammerman, Nancy Tatom. *Baptist Battles: Social Change and Religious Conflict in the Southern Baptist Convention*. New Brunswick, N.J.: Rutgers University Press, 1990.

Bellah, Robert N., et al. *Habits of the Heart: Individualism and Commitment in American Life.* Berkeley: University of California Press, 1985. Rev. ed., 1996.

Branch, Taylor. *Parting the Waters: America in the King Years, 1954–1963.* New York: Simon & Schuster, 1988.

———. *Pillar of Fire: America in the King Years, 1963–1965.* New York: Simon & Schuster, 1998.

Brandon, George. *Santeria from Africa to the New World: The Dead Sell Memories.* Bloomington: Indiana University Press, 1993.

Brown, Karen McCarthy. *Mama Lola: A Vodou Priestess in Brooklyn.* Berkeley: University of California Press, 1991.

Carpenter, Joel A. *Revive Us Again: The Reawakening of American Fundamentalism.* New York: Oxford University Press, 1997.

Eck, Diana L. *A New Religious America: How a "Christian Country" Has Become the World's Most Religiously Diverse Nation.* San Francisco: Harper, 2001.

Findlay, James F., Jr. *Church People in the Struggle: The National Council of Churches and the Black Freedom Movement, 1950–1970.* New York: Oxford University Press, 1993.

Fox, Richard Wightman. *Reinhold Niebuhr: A Biography.* New York: Pantheon, 1985.

Garrow, David. *Bearing the Cross: Martin Luther King, Jr., and the Southern Christian Leadership Conference.* New York: W. Morrow, 1986.

Gillis, Chester. *Roman Catholicism in America.* New York: Columbia University Press, 1999.

Hutchison William R., ed. *Between the Times: The Travail of the Protestant Establishment in America, 1900–1960.* New York: Cambridge University Press, 1989.

Kapur, Sudarshan. *Raising Up a Prophet: The African-American Encounter with Gandhi.* Boston: Beacon, 1992.

Lincoln, C. Eric, and Lawrence H. Mamiya. *The Black Church in the African-American Experience.* Durham, N.C.: Duke University Press, 1990.

Marty, Martin E. *Modern American Religion.* Vol. 1, *The Irony of It All, 1893–1919.* Chicago: University of Chicago Press, 1986. Vol. 2, *The Noise of Conflict, 1919–1941.* Chicago: University of Chicago Press, 1991. Vol. 3, *Under God, Indivisible, 1941–1960.* Chicago: University of Chicago Press, 1996.

McGreevy, John T. "Thinking on One's Own: Catholicism in the American Intellectual Imagination, 1928–1960." *Journal of American History* 84 (1997): 97–131.

———. *Catholicism and American Freedom: A History from Slavery to Today.* New York: Norton, 2003.

New International Dictionary of Pentecostal and Charismatic Movements. Edited by Stanley M. Burgess and Eduard van der Mass. Grand Rapids, Mich.: Zondervan, 2002.

Orsi, Robert A. *The Madonna of 115th Street: Faith and Community in Italian Harlem, 1880–1950.* New Haven, Conn.: Yale University Press, 1985.

———. *Thank You, St. Jude: Women's Devotion to the Patron Saint of Hopeless Causes.* New Haven, Conn.: Yale University Press, 1996.

Porterfield, Amanda. *The Transformation of American Religion: The Story of a Late Twentieth-Century Awakening.* New York: Oxford University Press, 2001.

Prothero, Stephen R. *American Jesus: How the Son of God Became a National Icon.* New York: Farrar, Straus & Giroux, 2003.

Roof, Wade Clark. *Spiritual Marketplace: Baby Boomers and the Remaking of American Religion.* Princeton, N.J.: Princeton University Press. 1999.

———, ed. *Contemporary American Religion.* New York: Macmillan, 2000.

Seager, Richard Hughes. *Buddhism in America.* New York: Columbia University Press, 1999.

Sernett, Milton C. *Bound for the Promised Land: African American Religion and the Great Migration.* Durham, N.C.: Duke University Press, 1997.

Smith, Jane I. *Islam in America.* New York: Columbia University Press, 1999.

Wuthnow, Robert. *After Heaven: Spirituality in America since the 1950s.* Berkeley: University of California Press, 1998.

Statistics

"Largest Religious Groups in the United States of America." http://www.adherents.com/rel_USA.html. Adherents.com, 2002.

Yearbook of American and Canadian Churches, 2002. Edited by Eileen W. Linder. Nashville, Tenn.: Abingdon, 2002.

Index

DAVID W. WILLS

is the Winthrop H. Smith '16 Professor of American History and
American Studies, and teaches in the departments of religion and
black studies at Amherst College.